BIBLICAL CHALLENGES FOR CHRISTIAN SINGLES

Jarvis L. Collier

Townsend 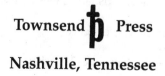 Press

Nashville, Tennessee

Printed in the U.S.A.
Published by the Townsend Press
Nashville, Tennessee

Library of Congress Catalog-in-Publication Data

Collier, Jarvis L.
    Biblical challenges for Christian singles / Jarvis L. Collier.
        p. cm.
    Includes bibliographical references.
    ISBN 0-910683-09-3
    1. Single people—Religious life. 2. Christian life—Biblical teaching.
I. Title.
BV4596.S5C65 1998   98-40579
248.8′4—dc21   CIP

Preface/Acknowledgments

The art of setting thoughts and concepts down in a systematic fashion, on a particular subject, with some degree of order, rationality and cogency is quite challenging. This is my first major attempt. I ask your indulgence for my errors and feeble efforts.

For some time, I have felt God stroking the creative embers within my heart and mind. By virtue of diverse ministry settings and fascinating encounters across America, I offer my reflections relative to Christian Singles ministry.

I am indebted to the wonderful members of the Fellowship Baptist Church, Los Angeles, California, for allowing me to initially preach and teach some of these concepts; as well, they have given me the freedom to pursue my calling in the area of writing for a larger audience.

Moreover, the many Singles groups I have addressed over the years have been veritable "laboratories" for developing biblically-based strategies for subsequent ministry. I sincerely appreciate their questions, observations, struggles, stories, tears and insights.

Various colleagues in ministry, across the country, will, no doubt, recognize their ideas here and there in the text. Professional, ministerial and ethical integrity cause me to acknowledge the need to properly assign sources to the thoughts of others. Yet, in some places, I may have inadvertently omitted such attribution, for which I apologize. You have my permission to take some of the material found here, even without the "footnote."

Please note also that this is a symphony with several parts left unfinished. In no way will it answer every question, for I know that Christian Singles are ever growing in their appropriation of biblical truth. This means that just when the "experts" discover the "true concerns" of Singles, they find that they were far off the mark. So, we continue the quest.

In this endeavor, I have been encouraged by a loving, supportive family, especially in the laughter and joy of my son, Jarvis II.

To God be the glory!

TABLE OF CONTENTS

INTRODUCTION

It should be apparent, from the data provided in official statistics of the United States Census, along with cursory observations, that Single Adults constitute a significant segment of the total population at large in this country.

In order to gain insight into the vast arena of Single life in America, let us consider the broad demographics peculiar to Singles.

In fact, over the age of 18, there are over 72 million Singles. Think of it, sometimes you feel so all alone!

The next time you go home to your family, ask yourself how many of your co-workers have gone home to a lonely apartment or condominium, constituting one in <u>39 million Single Adults who have never married.</u>

The next time you see someone eating alone in a restaurant, ask yourself if that person could be one of <u>14 million Single Adults</u> who have <u>experienced the death of a mate in the last year</u>.

The next time you watch five children at play, ask yourself if one of them lives in a single-parent household wherein <u>1 in 5 children under eighteen lives with a Single Adult Parent</u>. For black families, the number headed by a single parent, primarily female, approaches 60 per cent.

The next time you pass a health club or fitness center, ask yourself if the person coming out of the door could be one of <u>over 14 million Single Adults who divorced last year</u>.

What can we make of these sobering statistics? Are these Single Adults (because they have no mate) somehow strange? Deviant? Sick? Unusual? Maladjusted?

No - they are none of the above; rather, they simply show diverse faces woven into the tapestry of a world cloak, which all too often expresses a preference for a neat nuclear family consisting of the husband, wife, two children, a shaggy dog, and a pretty house with a white picket fence, thus fulfilling the prototypical American Dream!

You and I know, however, of thousands who do not fit this pattern; and we know that Single Adults are not strange, deviant, sick or unusual. They just happen to be Single.

Truth is, we must begin to celebrate Singlehood as a viable option, as a lifestyle. For the believer, it accords with the general principle of Scripture: "...Be content, in whatever state I am..." (Philippians 4:11).

The ethos dominant in America underscores a "marriage culture," as all signs point toward finding a mate before, so they say, "it's too late." Or, we hear, "Don't end up old and lonely." Or, "Can't you find somebody?" Or, "You must be too picky!" Or, "Don't you want to have kids?"

Such reminders of one's status come almost daily, from family and friends.

Single Adults come in many shapes and varieties. They happen to be our brothers, sisters, cousins, nephews, nieces, fathers, mothers and friends. They come from all walks of life (doctors, lawyers, dentists, pastors, plumbers, delivery drivers, nurses, carpenters, secretaries, flight attendants, clerks, salespersons, cops, etc.).

Most important, Single Adults are part of the human family for whom Jesus Christ, our Savior and Lord, shed His blood, for the remission of sin, for all who believe by faith.

Therefore, if the institutional church (over which Christ functions as Head) is to be relevant, practical, biblical and redemptive, we must have a renewed emphasis on ministry to the Single Adults.

Whether by <u>Decision</u>, <u>Divorce</u>, <u>Default</u>, <u>Death</u> (of a Spouse) or <u>Destiny</u>, the community of faith (the Church) must accept its God-ordained responsibility in reaching out to Single Adults.

The decision to remain in the Single grouping must be given merit, as many persons, such as nuns, priests, missionaries and committed Christians recognize a God-ordained challenge to live totally for Him, even if it means the prospect of not having a mate. The decision should be respected and the individual affirmed as a healthy decision to forego an important relationship for the faith they espouse toward the Lord.

Relative to divorce, according to those who have experienced it, there is a major life transition. Such persons' emotions run the gamut, from bitterness, anger, hurt, frustration, isolation, disorientation, loss, a sense of failure, betrayal, and a consequent determination never to make oneself vulnerable to another again in life. Not surprisingly, when the church seeks to minister in this arena, we must know something of the struggle one has in matters of trust and re-establishing one's emotional equilibrium.

For others, we may as well be blunt: some persons will never get married for a number of factors. It may be that the statistical imbalance of men and women precludes finding enough eligible persons. (Maybe it is more than a myth that some cities are just not filled with enough good men, to which each woman would reply, "I only need one!"). It may be that you will be overlooked because you have some standards in a mate, thus you will be forced to wait for the one who measures up. It may be that you intimidate others because of a false bravado that gives off the message that you are self-obsessed, indifferent to the wooing of another.

When it comes to the newly single, by virtue of a spouse's death, there is a deep sense of loss, accentuated by the quality of the relationship, the quantity of years spent together, the despair of ever having such intimacy again, the children brought forth and reared, the moments shared in joy together, the plans left unfinished, the dreams yet unexplored, and more. The grief process challenges the ministry to Singles because recovery will differ according to the circumstances briefly alluded to above.

The concept of destiny frightens many as it seems to describe some unalterable law of God, which comes without His love, whereby we are circumscribed to a life alone. The author does not mean such by the usage of the term destiny. Instead, in the plan of God, some are not to get married, for reasons He alone knows. Thus, to be married, is not the normative goal of life, but to glorify God in whatever state (relationally) one happens to occupy at the time.

For most writers and commentators, the specific period of life to which Single Adult Ministry speaks falls between the ages of 20-50ish. We know, at the same time, that there will be those well above any chronological cut off, who possess interest and spirit, thus no person should be excluded.

Furthermore, if the Single Adult in American society is to be reached with the gospel of Jesus Christ, we must know not only the gospel but who the Single Adult is who needs that gospel.

Today's Single Adult reads: *People, the Wall Street Journal, Newsweek, TIME, Entrepreneur, Ebony, Black Enterprise, Cosmopolitan, Playboy, Esquire, Architectural Digest, Success, Psychology Today, Essence, Gentlemen's Quarterly, "Women Who Love Too Much," "Good Women, Bad Choices," "Waiting to Exhale," "Women Who Run with Wolves," "Men are from Mars, Women are from Venus," the National Enquirer, Vanity Fair, Fortune, Forbes,* and at least two daily newspapers.

Today's Single Adult wears: Anne Klein II, Versace, Donna Karan, Liz Claiborne, Reeboks, Polo, LaCoste, Halston, Ann Taylor, Hugo Boss, Pierre Cardin, Calvin Klein, Nike Air Jordans, Brooks Brothers, London Fog, Gucci, Bijan, Giorgio, diamonds, and anything gold!

Today's Single Adult attends: the latest Eddie Murphy/ Denzel Washington/Wesley Snipes/Spike Lee movie, concerts of Whitney Houston, Toni Braxton, Luther Vandross, Rappers, Kool Jazz Festival, "happy hour" (a real misnomer!), dramas, plays, sporting events, openings, premieres, ballets, as many exciting events as possible, barbecues, pool parties, retreats, and recovery sessions for various needs.

Today's Single Adult saves for: a week of skiing in the mountains, a Carnival Cruise, a vacation in the Bahamas, Cancun, Aruba, Jamaica, or Hawaii, a Club Med Singles

Holiday, a new entertainment center, a CD player, a new leather sofa, a wide-screen television, a mink coat (treat oneself!), and a T-Bill or Money Market certificate.

Today's Single Adult <u>lives in</u>: a newly built condo, a spacious townhouse in an exclusive neighborhood, an apartment, a home with a "roommate" to whom he/she is not married, his/her parent's home, a state of high anxiety, with plans for the acquisition of a domicile of their own.

Today's Single Adult <u>thinks about</u>: the "biological clock" if not a mother by age 26-34, how beautiful/handsome others find them, a Mercedes Benz, Jaguar or Lexus while driving a Hyundai, financial independence while making $250.00 a week, the nuclear nightmare, whether he/she will ever find Mr./Ms. Right, the advantages of liposuction, the meaning of life, and how to be sane in a "crazy" world.

American trends, more and more, are shaped by the concerns of single Americans, as the marketplace seeks to satisfy their yearnings. It has been estimated that US firms project $200 billion in products, especially for the single lifestyle.

Clearly, to be Single is to be presented with a plethora of "things" with which to occupy oneself. Add to this the fact that Singles can buy indiscriminately and one begins to understand why advertisers target this segment of the populace. At the same time, we must face the reality that things will never fill the empty space. We will only find what is essential when we come to a faith relationship with the Lord Jesus Christ.

Such a profile reveals, again, the diversification among the masses of Single Adults in society, and, more especially, in the church. Since Singles differ so much, it behooves the body of Christ to shape a ministry with these differences in mind.

In a very related matter, the increased incidence of sexually-transmitted diseases has brought about a return to moral behavior; thus, bars and clubs have lost their allure as sights for discovering potential life partners.

(The venue in which a partner is found is directly related to the values by which an individual lives. If we seek one with godly values, we should search in the place where those with a reverence and affection for God go, namely, the church in its worships and ministries. While such a statement seems clear, far too many Christians, primarily but not limited to, females, lower their standards just to have "somebody" and end up with a spiritual "nobody." Again, the question is, "Where did you find your mate?" If at the job, you know you have a worker. If at school, you know you have one who appreciates learning. If at the church, you probably have one who loves the Lord. Of course, in everything there is an exception. Yet, the general rule holds that one ought seek a mate in a Christian setting, and the best site is still the Lord's House.)

The "Baby Boom" generation shows signs of greater conservatism in lifestyles, over against the promiscuity of the 60s, 70s, and early 80s. With the onset of AIDS, herpes and the like, in the latter 80s and into the 90s, the time is ripe for a re-evaluation of life choices. The year 2000 may very well usher in a full swing in the pendulum towards the family, the church, the school, the flag and the law as bulwarks of a new social order.

In this regard, Psalm 11 asks a pertinent question: "If the foundations (above) are destroyed, what can the righteous do?" The answer for the sincere Christian Single is to hold the banner of righteousness high as we evaluate potential life partners.

What are the Implications for Single Adult Ministry?

How can we create an environment for creative, practical, biblical ministry with an emphasis on a thriving relationship with Jesus Christ?

These questions and more will occupy our thoughts in this booklet on Single Adult Ministry.

Specificity dictates, then, the following breakdown among Single Adults:

A. Never Married, College Students (18-26)

B. Never Married, Career Singles (27-50ish)

C. Divorced Singles, Separated Singles

D. Widowed, Recovering Singles

E. Single Parents

Of course, there will be some overlap among the groups. Whatever the case, the intent is to organize so as to allow for those with similar life situations to share their needs.

Early on, if there is to be a biblical foundation to undergird our efforts, we need to affirm that Single Adults are integral parts of the biblical witness to the redemptive work of God in history.

Note well the "<u>Notable Never Married</u>" in Scripture:

Hagar - the danger of a rash judgment; single parent
*   - Genesis 21*
Deborah - the life of a forever "bridesmaid"
*   - Genesis 24; 35*
Dinah - youthful indiscretions can color future choices
*   - Genesis 34*
Miriam - co-leader of Israel; Moses' sister - Exodus 15
Rahab - a harlot used by God - Joshua 2;6
Elijah - God's man on the go - 1 Kings 17
Jeremiah - single by God's command - Jeremiah 16:1-9
Daniel - man of strong faith - Daniel 1; 6:10
Daughters of Philip - vocal evangelists - Acts 21:8-9
John the Baptizer - forerunner of the Redeemer
*   - Matthew 3; Luke 1*
Jesus Christ - Savior and Lord - Luke 8
Mary Magdalene - out of whom demons were cast - Luke 8
Mary, Martha and Lazarus - friends of the Messiah - John 11
Dorcas - a faithful worker for godly causes - Acts 9
Paul - apostle to the Gentiles - 1 Corinthians 7
Many others unnamed in the Bible.

Thus, we can see a conspicuous concern for the needs of Single Adults in the plan of God. In every case sighted above, the persons were dedicated, godly, energetic, useful and committed to leading others to a salvific knowledge of God.

A word needs to be said in response to one who expressed a negative attitude toward Single Adult Ministry (ironically, even as she was in the cohort group for it).

A. Some view Single Adult Ministry as a "meat market," where Singles come to meet others, with the goal of marriage in the future.

B. Others conceive of Single Adult Ministry as a sounding board for gripes, in the "I-can-top-your-story" format.

C. Still others resent Single Adult Ministry because it calls attention to that segment in the church membership which as no partner for life.

In designing a Ministry, we must be careful to steer clear of such fears and concerns. Instead, the life of a Single Adult must be seen as healthy, wholesome, fulfilling, exciting and creative.

In the pages to follow, we shall endeavor to discuss the biblical responses to contemporary issues relative to Single Adults. As we know that every imaginable challenge of life will be faced during these years, it stands to reason that we all need reliable principles for our decisions.

We hope to cover the gamut of issues for Single Adults at this epic moment in human history, as we stand at the dawning of the 21st Century, fraught with new stresses and novel strains.

"God's Call On Your Life" examines the basis of a relationship with Jesus Christ, which must characterize the life of a successful Single Adult. Attention will be given to the meaning of a serious commitment to God as it will impact all other relationships.

"An Alternative to Anxiety" will explore the simple proposition that God does, in deed, care about all, particularly, Single Adults. In this gigantic world, as many live in crowded places, amidst millions, one can get lost. The songwriter asked the question, "Does Jesus Care?" We hope to give an affirmative and triumphant answer to the inquiry.

"_The Search for Simplicity_" issues forth in a call for a life of fellowship with God in daily devotion and quiet meditation on the Scripture, with the intent of application for every facet of life. Singles should view this period in their lives as a time to focus on finding the will of God. Christ should be the center around which all of life revolves. This "centering" occurs in a daily discipline of prayer and meditation. Something grand develops from time spent in conversation with Him. If there is to be "depth" in the walk of faith, it will only come about as one meets God in prayer.

"_Self Imagery_" asks and hopefully answers some important inquiries into how Singles view themselves. A healthy self-image allows for a long life of contentment with the station set by God. The emphasis will be on gaining insight into the Master's original intent, so as to know who we are by His evaluation. Depending upon the vantage point from which one is viewed, we are able to know our place in life.

"_Human Sexuality_" begins with the creative purpose of God and takes us through the current topics relative to physical, psychological and social development. At the same time, we hope to assess what, from a Christian standpoint, can only be termed "perversions" of that divine ideal for human sexual function. No matter that "everybody's doing it," the believer uses a different standard of judgment.

"_Looking in the Mirror_" will be an earnest attempt to provide a practical word to all as Singles focus on improving self, to the extent each is capable. The reasoning is clear: improve self, and others will be attracted. Far more than improvements in the exterior (new hairdo, the loss of a few pounds, a visit to the gym, new contact lens, etc.) will be addressed. In fact, the best improvement comes in the work we must do in the interior space. All the rest is but "cosmetic."

"_Interpersonal Relationships_" will develop the horizontal

aspect of our lives, including relating to "significant" and "insignificant" others. Since friends shape our thinking, assist us in the organization of our grand plans and thoughts, share with us life's vicissitudes, and become surrogate family members in many cases, we need to examine friendship. Also, friends and platonic relationships furnish the antidote for loneliness. Thus, who are our friends and why are they so important? This chapter will delve into the matter.

"_Foundations for Marriage_" will be a detailed analysis of the full teaching of Scripture on an area of interest to Single Adults, many of whom have "fantasy" concepts of marital commitment. There will be a synthesis of the biblical material and popular, clinical counseling techniques.

"_Mate Selection_" offers several suggestions as to how one should go about searching for that partner for life. Maturity and prayer are two key concepts for this search.

"_Rebounding and Rebuilding_" will move towards a redemptive word for those coming out of failed relations as the healing takes place in an atmosphere of love and acceptance. We will not sugar-coat the truth: life has some hurtful places. A bad relationship must be viewed as a part of the human experience. Each episode should be taken as a learning experience. No matter that one falls down, we serve a God who majors in giving His own greater strength when they arise!

"_Career Development_" will speak to the need for a place in the world as one seeks gainful employment in the American marketplace. Gainful employment is necessary for economic security, thus, the intent will be to share practical insights for advancement in one's career. Whenever people spend eight-plus hours somewhere, 52 weeks a year, with few benefits, for 25 years, with the hope of a pension, we need to be sure that such an expenditure of time and spirit has purpose.

"_The Matter of My Money_" begins a dialogue which should eventuate in a way of life of harmony and blessedness in the areas of time, talent and treasure. Your money is a barometer of your faith. How do you spend it? By your allocations, you announce who is really lord in your life. Money is not filthy or a personal issue. God has something to say about it which every Single Adult needs to hear.

"*Hagar: Portrait of a Single Mother*" aims to speak to those within our churches who need affirmation and love for their untiring work and sacrifices to maintain a healthy home environment in the absence of a two parent household. Particularly is the issue germane in the African American community as so many women must play dual roles because of the paucity of fathers on the landscape.

"*Drug Abuse*" challenges those who have given themselves over to the most deadly external threat known to man at this hour. The Christian community must declare in loud tones the fact that drug abuse is no cure for what ails many Single Adults. The "high" extracts too great a price on one's good name, character, family, potential and more. Again, life has to be lived with an awareness of Christ, as He becomes the coping mechanism for the "craziness" all about us.

"*Where Christian Singles Gather*" offers a panoply of hints as to finding a mate and enjoying healthy opportunities for fellowship. If there is one question this writer has been asked more than a few times, it has been, "Well, where can we find the kind of Christian men/women you describe in this book?" So, as a beginning answer, I offer a few proven suggestions. To be sure, the right person may be right under your nose, so to speak.

"*How to Develop a Christian Singles Ministry*" comes from several years of gleaning the best of many successful ministries across America, as I have been invited many places. There are many similarities in the Single life, thus we propose to assess several of these dynamic efforts. We need not "reinvent the wheel" in designing a ministry. Where we can learn from others, we must. I have also discovered that racial, denominational, class and economic differences mean very little, for Single Adult Ministry seeks to answer the same needs.

"*The Future*" explores the challenges ahead for Single Adults in all areas of human endeavor.

At the end of this study, we pray that many Single Adults will find that the Ministry offers an interesting and exhilarating means of learning and doing during the period of singlehood - whether it lasts throughout life or results in marriage.

Most important in this regard is the goal of an on-going Ministry, rather than a few weeks of emphasis. Build a ministry that focuses on people. Build a ministry that is holistic. Build a ministry that is thoroughly spiritual and spirited. Build a ministry whereby people will look forward to the gathering. Build a ministry for all Singles. Build a ministry with built-in blessing for the total church family.

GOD'S CALL ON YOUR LIFE

The operative question for our time asks, "What is God up to?" It should not surprise anyone that the Lord God is, in fact, active in the created order. He loves humanity and carries a conspicuous concern for His creatures.

As Single Adults, the question often arises, "Does anyone really care?" This chapter seeks to answer in the affirmative, for we have a caring God, One who does not sit on some remote throne, totally disconnected from His creation. Instead, He is a pro-active, seeking Heavenly Father.

From the earliest moments of human history, in that idyllic Garden, in the Genesis account, we discover One who yet loves Adam and Eve, even after their disobedience. He will not leave them alone, even as their sinful acts separate them from Him. He makes the distinction between the sinful act (which He hates) and the sinful person (whom He loves with an eternal love).

In a simple declaration, John 3:16 states, "For God so loved the world, that he gave his only begotten Son, that whosoever believeth in him should not perish, but have everlasting life."

That's it! That's what God is up to!

He desires a redemptive relationship of love and guidance for every person who accepts Jesus Christ (His Son) by personal belief and trust.

The key word here is "relationship," which involves two persons sharing one with the other. Each gives a part of himself/herself. Each receives from the other. Each will have his/her needs met.

Notice that I have not broached the word "religion," because to accept Jesus Christ as one's personal Savior and Lord can in no wise be referred to as "religion." The difference here is far greater than some semantic splitting of hairs. Rather, to accept Christ is the beginning of a redemptive relationship, with life and vitality.

Religion is cold, sterile adherence to a set of rules laid down by some human leader who seeks to utilize concepts and dogma to reign in partisans who share common beliefs. In fact, religion is man-made as an attempt to reach up to some notion of God with an emphasis on good works.

What we find as one comes into a relationship differs markedly. The dominant motif is the reaching down of God toward humanity, precisely because the sinful nature of humanity would altogether render it unable to ever please the holiness of God. Therefore, God sent His own Son!

In this new relationship, God grants forgiveness, love, acceptance, access to the throne of grace, and the joy of peace. Man, on the other hand, gives praise, loyalty, allegiance, obedience and his "all" to the One who gave His Son in the first place.

1. What prevents the relationship, of course, is man's sinful condition.

Read Romans 3:23 and explain its affect on your life.

Sin can be defined by several concepts: missing the mark; violation of the law of God; imputed unrighteousness from Adam to all mankind; selfishness to a perverse end; a natural capacity to carry out that which is counter to the will and way of God.

Even in our enlightened, sophisticated day, I still dare to call sin by its rightful name. There is no hope in seeking to justify some of the acts that take place. Sin is very real. It motivates, dominates, captivates and separates. It causes us to act in ways that displease the Father. It reveals the inescapable reality of our root self-centeredness.

Often I ask, "Whatever happened to sin?"

Too many consider the word a quaint concept better left in Sunday school and childhood; yet, I still assert that sin is a reality for adults!

Sin ruins lives by the millions. Sin causes deep regret. Sin injures the human psyche by instilling a sense of guilt. Sin puts people on psychiatric couches. Sin breaks up families. Sin lies at the root of incest in families. Sin robs so many of their potential. Sin leads many down a path of wasted living by drug abuse, alcohol and violence. Sin is very real.

2. In addition, God takes sin seriously.

Read Romans 6:23 and explain its affect on your life.

Just as every act has an equal and opposite reaction, so too does the idea prevail in reference to sin. God pays the sinner, but, unfortunately, the wage is death.

Death in this context refers to eternal separation from God in a place called Hell (Luke 16:23), a real place without any exit. Yes, this writer believes in a literal place called hell! Yes, a loving God can consign individuals to that place, because it must also be remembered that God is also just, which means, among other things, that He has to uphold His own code of holiness and righteousness.

(Parenthetically, allow me to add that people will not go to hell because they were sinful and committed all sorts of heinous acts. No, people will face the prospect of hell for just one reason: they have not accepted the plan of God found in His Son Jesus Christ.)

3. <u>To spare us such an awful outcome, God gave a wonderfully simple example of unmerited agape (love from God) toward all.</u>

Read Romans 5:8 and explain its affect on your life.

What is most astounding here is the unlikely way the love of God was displayed: the most unlikely <u>people</u> ("us"), the most unlikely <u>period</u> ("while we were yet sinners"), offering the most unlikely <u>person</u> ("Christ"), asking for the most unlikely <u>provision</u> ("died").

Yet, this was and is precisely the method of God for mankind. What trips up so many is the utter simplicity of the plan of salvation. Had the Lord God made it complex and mysterious, many would have been drawn to Him, as if on the basis on human reckoning and exertion. Instead, He chose to relate to humanity in a simple fashion: through the incarnation (coming in flesh) of Jesus Christ.

4. Personal salvation, the basis for a relationship with God, comes as we ask in faith in Jesus Christ.

Read Romans 10:9 and explain its affect on your life.

"Confess" means to declare openly, to affirm, to agree, to announce to any within hearing range. When a person truly comes to Jesus Christ for personal salvation, he/she comes with a strong confidence in the new faith. It stands to reason that we confess what we believe, as well as we often believe what we confess.

We do well to recognize the difference between "belief" in the sense of intellectual assent, which means very little in the way of personal salvation, as one can observe many aspects of creation, without recognizing the unique God behind them. Scripture even teaches that the devil/demons believe and tremble; yet, such belief does not alter his condition.

Thus, when we refer to the basis of confession, we mean such a belief that one is staking a definite claim to the Lordship of Jesus Christ in a way that means He deserves unequaled allegiance and loyalty.

Moreover, what an individual confesses to in faith is not merely words. The confession involves all of one's life and exhibits itself in a changed lifestyle. The believer becomes a new convert, with a new dynamic at work within. 2 Corinthians 5:17 describes such a person as a "new creature."

5. <u>As an indication of eternal security, ultimately in the promise of God, we have a word for future days</u>.

Read Romans 8:1 and explain its affect on your life.

No condemnation carries the connotation of a person sentenced to life imprisonment, who suddenly hears from the warden that he is totally free, as all charges have been dropped! (Jesus Christ, on Calvary, took the "condemnation" for us!).

From the above, then, we should accept as truth the love of God for all humanity, as He seeks to bring the totality of His creation into the orbit of divine acceptance, as the Scriptures underscore His compassion. He is not desirous of any individual's perishing, none need be estranged from Him (2 Peter 3:9), and all can come to repentance.

A word needs to be said about the all-inclusive nature of the word "all." No one is beyond it. No one is too sinful, too bad, too mean, too lost, or too anything, that the loving hand of the Lord Jesus Christ cannot reach. We must hear this urgent appeal!

Therefore, we must begin any Single Adult Ministry with the emphasis placed on the necessity of a dynamic relationship with God, through the Savior and Lord, Jesus Christ.

Perhaps before we move into activities, we need to determine the spiritual condition of all who express an interest in the Ministry. There is a definite place in Singles Ministry gatherings for an appeal for new converts because some persons may attend who have yet to pray a prayer of faith.

In times like these, the church and its leadership cannot take for granted that any of its congregants has a commitment to Christ.

<u>The leader of the Single Adult Ministry should, therefore, be one who has demonstrated a high degree of spiritual maturity, as well as the capacity to lead others in the discovery of new levels of spiritual growth</u>.

He/she should know, in short, what God is up to and how one can get involved in a life-changing relationship with Him.

6. <u>The major part of the relationship with Christ begins at the point of initial salvation and continues throughout life</u>.

Read Romans 5:1-5 and explain its affect on your life.

<u>Salvation</u> is step one; <u>Sanctification</u> is step two; and <u>Glorification</u> consummates the relationship in heaven.

Step one has already been given by Christ. All that was required for the salvation of every individual was consummated in Christ. When He uttered those words from the Cross, "It is finished," He was referring to the plan of human redemption, rather than stating His own plans. In a word, He is not yet finished!

Step two focuses on the plan of God for Christian growth.

<u>Spiritual Growth occurs in the context of the following</u>: a daily period of prayer; regular fellowship with other believers; study and application of the principles derived from Scripture; a commitment to the life of New Testament discipleship; a lifestyle in which one is accountable to another believer; consistent support of the church by means of tithes/offerings; sharing of one's faith with the lost and unchurched; and openness to the leading of the Holy Spirit.

Step three awaits our eternal rest with God in heaven, thus, may we content ourselves with the brief sketches drawn from Holy Writ (read Revelation) as to what awaits the believer.

In this way, we see that a Single Adult Ministry undergirds the total work of the church, as well as seeking to reach those of a particular age grouping.

Yet, the wise person will keep the focus on what God seeks, rather than simply to engage in a secular fellowship or support group for persons with similar needs.

The way to ensure a "spiritual" Ministry is to get "spiritual" persons at the forefront and all throughout the Ministry. Anything less will mean compromise in the work which lies ahead.

Having said the above, at great length, dear reader, the question is, "Have you come to the place in life where you have accepted Jesus Christ as your personal Savior and Lord?"

If you had to meet God, could you meet Him without fear? If you were to die tonight, would you have a basis upon which to be granted entrance into heaven?

Remember, good works, keeping the Ten Commandments, treating everybody right, being as good as the next person, trying to live right, and anything else is not sufficient to get you into heaven.

The only way to reach the Father in peace is that you come to Him by His Son Jesus Christ (He is central to the idea of salvation and righteousness with God (John 14:6).

(Before going any further, my friend, please take my advice. Pray this prayer with me: "Lord Jesus, I confess my sin before You. I ask that You come into my heart and take control of my life. I own You as my Savior. Teach me Your word and allow me to learn more of You. Thank You for salvation. In Your name. Amen.")

(If you mean what you said, the Bible declares that you are saved, now and forever! As quickly as you possibly can, make contact with another believer in Christ. Ask such a friend or family member to pray with you. At the first opportunity, seek for a fellowship of believers (a church family) and ask God to lead you into the particular body of believers where you may grow in Him. The best criteria for a church family is one where the Word of God is preached and taught as the authoritative standard for faith and life.)

AN ALTERNATIVE TO ANXIETY

First Peter 5:7 should be a passage committed to memory by those who seek some degree of equilibrium amidst the shifting sands of this life. Specifically, the words of that awesome text are quite simple, yet profound: "... casting all your anxiety (care) upon Him, because He cares for you."

Psychiatrists and psychologists, not to mention self-help authors, would lose their business overnight if more people could simply appropriate the truth of the above passage from Scripture. In one full swoop, many would move toward emotional wholeness, as a product of recognition of the power of such an assertion from the Holy Writ. Thus, most of us would conserve time, money and stress, if only we could believe that, in fact, "He cares for me!"

As Christian Singles traverse through life, keen to the uncertainties of each day, gripped by concerns foreign to those who are married, the above cited passage can serve to mediate many frustrations.

Let the thread of hope run throughout this chapter: God cares! About me! He really does! No matter the test, He cares!

What an astounding, awe-inspiring concept, that the God of the universe, the Creator, the Sustainer, the Almighty One, the Great I AM is concerned with the plight of all humanity - including, and especially, those who happen to be Single.

Nothing occurs on the human plane without His notice. So, believe it, my friend, your life matters a great deal to the Master. He created you, gave life to you, endowed you, blessed you, sent His Son Jesus Christ to save you, filled you with the Holy Spirit, and is permanently in you to guide you. After having done all that for you, does it not stand to reason that He would be aware of your station in life?

The Apostle Peter, while writing to the entirety of the body of Christ (the Church), tells each believer of God's unstinting, non-negotiable concern for every aspect of our lives. He does so by giving a binding promise.

God is truly concerned about our hopes, our faith, our dreams, our habits, our frustrations, our stresses, our daily steps, our choices in life, our careers, our mates (or lack thereof), our sense of purpose, our conversations, and our character.

God is also concerned about our tears, our questions, our lonely moments, our doubts, our lack of enthusiasm, our temper tantrums when He seems to delay, our lack of trust when He seems otherwise occupied, our moves before He gives the go-ahead, and our child-like tendency to bring Him the shattered pieces of our lives.

In short, God is totally, fully, definitively concerned about us!

Allow the truth to settle on your heart, mind and spirit, like the morning dew, refreshing the soil of your inner being: "God cares!"

One contemporary lyricist said it well, in the words, "It Matters to Him About Me."

Another asked the question, in a melodic fashion, "Does Jesus Care?" The awesome refrain out of glory calls out, "O, Yes, He Cares!"

For the believer, the Savior went to Calvary because He cares; He is seated at the right hand of the Father interceding for the saints because He cares; He dispatched the Holy Spirit to guide us because He cares; and we anticipate His return because He cares.

Once we establish in our thinking that He cares, the First Peter 5 passage encourages Christian Singles further by giving a needed piece of advice: cast all anxiety upon Him.

The One who has repeatedly shown His ability to handle anxiety is the Father. Thus, we can and must "cast" or "throw" our anxiety upon His stout and steady shoulders that He may demonstrate anew, for us, His love and care.

If we cast such anxiety upon the Lord, it will alleviate the necessity of calling friends and family, for they are unable to root out the "source" of the anxiety, which is doubt about our place in the scheme of God's design. Too often, psychologists and self-help books only touch the "symptoms" and totally miss the "cause" of the emotional malady. As a result, we are left stressed out, anxious, tired and on the edge.

In point of fact, too many Christian Singles are caught in a difficult position of being full of anxiety about conditions they can do very little about. One's marital status should always be a matter of serious prayer and waiting before God. When we move before He gives the spiritual "greenlight," we face the danger of one of life's "moving violations," often called bad relationship, resentment, separation or divorce.

So far we have discussed anxiety without actually developing an adequate definition of it. In order to proceed further, we need one.

Anxiety is "an over-arching preoccupation with future issues and scenarios beyond one's capacity to control or capability to change." Or "concern respecting some event which disturbs the mind and keeps it in a state of painful uneasiness." Or "a state of restlessness and agitation of the mind, accompanied by a distressing sense of pressure in the vicinity of the heart."

Anxiety, from these definitions, touches the total person: emotional (heart), mental (mind), and volitional (will) dimensions. It impacts how we feel, how we reason, and how we act.

To be sure, at some time or another, everybody has some anxiety about something. It may be one's prospects for a job, the advisability of purchasing a home or automobile, an impending crisis in family, or a hundred things.

Serious spiritual and emotional problems develop, however, to the degree that one allows such concerns to debilitate proper functioning in the times leading up to the major decision or situation we must face. We use the pejorative term "nervous breakdown" to describe one who has a very serious inability to cope with one of life's major adjustments. One may require clinical and professional assistance to face such a situation.

Yet, it bears repeating that too many Christian Singles live lives on "hold," awaiting some form of validation from a relationship. So, all the while leading up to it, they are what one would term "anxious."

At this point we need to hear the Gospel writer, Matthew, chapter 6, in particular, for therein we have an instructive periscope of Scripture. He could have been leading a seminar on Singles Ministry when he addressed the issue of anxiety.

The areas of anxiety he speaks of, along with the ones contemporary life elucidate, fall under the headings: Food; Fame; Friends; Fashion; Fitness; Fortune; Future; and Focus.

As you peruse the above list, you will discover the entire gamut of concerns. In any one area there is the potential for much anxiety and mental disquiet. We often are pushed and pulled in many directions by our concerns in any one area.

For the believer, the best antidote for the malady of anxiety comes as one sharpens the focus of concern to seeking the kingdom of God, which means that the "King" will have full "dominion" in your heart and life. When He has such freedom, such latitude in your affairs (literally and figuratively), He will bring order to the chaos of your emotions.

(Far too many persons divide life into two zones: 1) areas for God to control {faith, prayer, Bible study, church attendance, etc.} and 2) areas where they must hold sway

{career, finances, mate selection, deciding to terminate pregnancies, where to live, etc.}; but, in actuality, everything
about which we process options ought to be a serious matter of prayer before the Lord.)

When there is a laser-like focus on kingdom priorities,
the Father will demonstrate His ability to align our lives.
Maybe the barometer of what our priorities happen to be is
not what we say they are, but whether there is symmetry in
our inner person.

To further assure the saint, especially the Single one,
the Apostle Paul weighs in on the topic of anxiety in
Philippians 4. Again, the Gospel Globetrotter, himself
Single, calls all to a place of "rest" in the Master.

In Philippians 4:6, we discover a Greek word
"merimnate" for our English word "anxiety." In the original Greek, the understanding was "to draw in different directions, to be distracted," which conveys the sense of what
occurs in the heart and mind of one so afflicted.

Too many attractive, handsome, intelligent, healthy,
well-off persons attend our churches, week after week,
appearing to be whole on the outside, yet hurting on the
inside, distracted by an intense desire for a mate, a life
partner, when God seeks that same person to find his/
her focus in Him.

When we operate outside the plan/will of God, even in
the anxiety-filled world of mate selection (a separate chapter), we face continual frustration, dead-end relationships,
and soap-opera commitments. Our lives become fodder for
the numerous television talk-shows, even as there is no real
healing in our lives.

The text of Philippians 4 reveals that there are two possibilities, two paths open before us: 1) pray, or 2) be anxious. That's it! No other options!

Please do not allow the simplicity of prayer to prevent
you from doing it.

Those who are prayerful about everything need be anxious about nothing!

Those who are prayerful about nothing are anxious about everything!

We must hasten to add that prayer in these mundane areas (such as career, mate, major decisions, and more) is just as critical as what we would term more "spiritual" issues. In short, the operative thesis must be that all of life, for the Christian, is "spiritual," because without the leading of God's Spirit we are set adrift in a sea of concerns.

When we pray over such critical matters, we gain hold of a powerful peace, in our inner spirit, which settles us, which takes away the anxiety, replacing it with a capacity we cannot understand, let alone those around us.

Our minds are guarded against the "enemy" called anxiety by God's peace, which this world cannot and will not ever understand. Without Christ in their lives, neither will friends, family or co-workers understand it. In fact, they will ask some questions.

Surely, you have heard their questions: "Aren't you concerned about getting a husband/wife?" "Don't you care that you don't have children by now?" "Why are you letting your life get away?" "Are you trying to "land" somebody?"

Such questions make it plain that they don't know the Source of your peace, for when you put the concern in the hand of the Lord, you must leave it there. Let Him take the time you need (no misprint there) to prepare you for it. Yes, my friend, more than likely God delays in delivering what we ask in order to develop us in that which we ask. He works both in us and the person or situation He prepares us for.

Without leaving the passage of Philippians 4, God enjoins us, through Paul, to "let your requests be made known to God." In a word, be specific in your prayer posture. There is nothing so sad, so defeatist, so wimpy as one who always says, with resignation and defeat, "let your will be done."

(Quickly, we must understand that the believer should

always pray with the will of God uppermost in mind. However, if we only pray an innocuous, generic, bland "thy will be done" type prayer, then we will not be prepared to praise God as He answers a specific prayer request.)

If it's a mate you desire, go to God in earnest about such. Pour out your heart to Him. Give even some features you desire in that individual. There is no need for "posturing" because, after all, God knows even the intents of your heart. The more specific you are, the easier it will be to recognize one as heaven sent.

Again, it bears repeating: the timing of God's answer to our request is left solely with Him, for "He cares" for each of us.

God's will for each person is as unique as the fingerprint and can be discerned as He engages us in prayer, study of His Word, the prompting of the Holy Spirit, the wisdom and counsel of mature persons in the body of Christ, and lectures/tapes/books by Christian authors.

Over and again, the Christian Single is admonished to take comfort in the above-cited passages, to gain insight in the area of combating anxiety.

Whatever the source of the anxiety, no matter how extreme, no matter that it has been a source of stress and mental disquiet, those in the family of God have abundant resources at hand.

Finally, too many persons in the Christian walk give up on God, taking matters into their own hands, without realizing that God had already signed the "requisition form" for your blessing!

When the anxiety quotient rises, you have a spiritual means of reaching a state where that matter is in the Master's hand. Glory to His name!

THE SEARCH FOR SIMPLICITY

In the hustle and bustle of contemporary living, especially in a big city, as noise blares from every side, as we run here and there in an endless search for true fulfillment. I am reminded of the harried refrain of the song, "Stop the World, I Want to Get Off!"

Far too many persons, in their 30s, 40s and early 50s are succumbing to heart failure, stress is the byword, and often the root of the malady is the speed at which we are operating this fragile vehicle called the human life.

At the same time, young people are giving off "mixed messages" as they seem so old. Gray hairs dot the heads of youngsters. (Don't tell me about "prematurely gray" or "character" and please don't try to fool us with that dye job!) The truth is that we are moving way too fast along the vast stretches of the landscape.

It seems as if the world moves about at a fever-pitched pace. In this frantic environment, <u>we set speed records on a treadmill</u>! The chief problem being that we really never get anywhere, although we try hard.

In the movie, Mahogany, the question was asked of Diana Ross, as she raced to capture Europe as a fashion designer, turning her back on family, friends, love and values of a lifetime, "<u>Do you know where you're going to?</u>" Some Single Adults need to hear that question.

Everyone we meet has the same problem: stress. It describes both personal and societal reality, and ranks alongside other bona fide reasons for absence and disabilities in the workplace. We are no longer able to manage our high pressure jobs, even though we make much more money, have bigger, more comfortable offices, enjoy greater "perks" and benefits, take longer vacations, demand better conditions and purchase more expensive "things."

Somehow, something has gone terribly wrong! It's just too complex!

How do we cope? How do we handle life, without resorting to mindless drug addiction, harmful liaisons/affairs, and fatalistic thinking?

The problem is yet acute in light of the <u>institutional decay</u> we see all about us. Perhaps we must engage in a contemporary dialogue with the Psalmist, who raised a crucial rhetorical point in Psalm 11:3, "<u>If the foundations be destroyed, what can the righteous do</u>?"

We are now in the generation where the conditional "if" has been replaced by the damning "when", for foundations are crumbling all about us!

Notice the critical concerns which raise their voices and call out to our attention.

Is the flag really a symbol for freedom, justice, equality and the chance to succeed in a land where character supersedes color? Does the United States Constitution, the Bill of Rights, the United States Supreme Court, and the principle of justice resonate in your heart and mind? Is justice real or is it "just us" with people of African heritage left unprotected? Do you still pledge your allegiance to the "Red, White and Blue?" Does the National Anthem touch you personally?

Is the family endangered by the fact that we attend many weddings which may never become marriages? How cynical are you about the supposed "happy marriages" you view? Can the family still make a difference when so many seem so sad, when they remain as such? When they break apart, what does this say for building healthy homes and strong character traits for the future? Are "headship" (for the husband) and "submission" (for the wife) valid concepts when feminists call upon a new order in the family? Are the talk-shows right in parading family feuds before their viewing audiences? Is the new word "dysfunctional" the best one to describe most families?

Is the church a spiritual body, with Jesus Christ as her head, salvation for her end, the Holy Spirit as her guide and love for her witness. Or, is she only a social gathering for the moral and upright? Can a forgiving spirit be found within her walls? Can I bring my broken heart, my fractured self-image, my wasted years, my hurt and despair within her confines? Is there any "balm" therein for the bruises of this callous world? When I arrive at the sacred place, will anybody care to know my name or to address me as a person, rather than another body? Will the people of God embrace me as a sister or a brother? How long must I remain a stranger, when we all name the name of Christ as our shared Lord?

Are schools venues for the acquisition of mental tools and techniques or merely holding pens for the illiterate? Where do we send our children that they may come out as productive, prepared persons, able to make a contribution to the world? Do we live amidst those who would rather imprison young talent due to foolish decisions, rather than educate precious minds and uncertain hearts?

You may ask, "What does this mean to Single Adult Ministry?"

My answer involves the search for the simple life of meditation and prayer to God for answers to these perplexities, which keep us in motion though we never gain a sense of movement.

In our hurried moments, we have lost sight of the simple path, thus we have lost our Creator and the connection we need to Him.

May I propose that we forget the spotlights, escape the pulsating beat, turn down the volume (literally and figuratively), close the door, and get quiet for special moments of interior development. Most of us have it together on the outside, but inside we face chaos.

This chapter is a call for "redecorating the interior space." In this case, you need not call another in for their ideas on color, fabric, moods or what goes where. This redecoration entails getting alone with the Master as He seeks to declare what must remain and what must be discarded.

Allow me to introduce you to a man who successfully

engaged in the arduous task of slowing down, so as to focus on the interior space. He describes his journey in the Old Testament hymn book, which we refer to as Psalms. If you can, open the Word of God to Psalm 131 and walk with our tour guide as he directs us through his interior space.

(While we rummage through David's interior space, I must caution that it will get a bit messy, but I don't think he will mind the intrusion, so long as you and I recognize that a similar trek through our own space will reveal the same muck and mess.)

Psalm 131 will be the basis for this call to simplicity because every Single Adult (and every believer in Christ, for that matter) must keep this uppermost in mind, if there is to be coping with the "traffic" of the contemporary lifestyle.

Psalm 131 is a "quiet" and "simple" bit of praise. Loudness is a foreign concept to this writer. Frenetic movement has been cast away in favor of a "settled spirit." To read this passage is to lower the speed at which most people accomplish tasks.

Hear the words of this "Song of Ascents," penned by David, king of Israel.

> O, Lord, my heart is not proud, nor my eyes haughty;
> Nor do I involve myself in great matters,
> Or in things too difficult for me.
> Surely I have composed and quieted my soul;
> Like a weaned child rests against his mother,
> My soul is like a weaned child within me.
> O, Lord, hope in the Lord
> From this time forth and forever.

<u>David makes an astounding declaration of faith: the simple life can be found in the quiet place of a person's yielded spirit</u>.

The route to such a state, however, turns away from the noise, the traffic, the glaring, klieg lights, the pulsating beat, the thumping rhythms, the boisterous crowds and the lightning speeds.

Although he is the head of state, the reigning monarch, the sweet singer, the mighty warrior, David still operates with a deep awareness of the need for communication with his true source: Jehovah God.

When tempted to make the excuse of being "too busy" to pray (Read Bill Hybels book so named), remember all that David had with which to cope. Despite it all, the king knew that he had to call upon God for "centering."

Do you stop to call on God? Do you ask His guidance for the tremendous and the trivial? Do you recognize the need for a moment of focus, when the walls begin to close in?

(If not, put this book down right now, and talk to God in earnest prayer.)

Consider what others have done. In 1845, Henry David Thoreau, essayist and poet, built a tiny cabin beside Walden Pond in Concord, Massachusetts. Here he lived in utter simplicity for two years. A small cabin, away from the city, became his means of escape. He needed to quiet his soul!

The Winans, a Detroit-based contemporary gospel group, wrote and gave to the world a song entitled, "<u>Secret Place</u>" with the emphasis on getting alone with God in meditation and prayer.

In the New Testament, Matthew 17, the disciples of Christ encountered a situation beyond their capacity to cope: a boy with a demon. They tried valiantly to call the demon out, as Jesus had given them power to do in earlier times. On this occasion, however, they were failures. Upon questioning the Master as to the reason for the spiritual "power outage," they discovered a lack. No, not a lack in the power of God. No power lack in Christ. No power lack in the Holy Spirit.

The disciples, so said the Lord Jesus, failed because they didn't pray!

Mystics of all stripes have left the trappings of society to find a remote locale for the purpose of communing unhindered with the Lord of life.

You can, nevertheless, remain in the society, but remain aloof from its trappings. You can quiet your spirit even as the noise goes on all about you.

All of the above are examples of the necessity of finding a "sanctuary" amidst the complexity of the day to meet with the Maker.

<u>Call it "quiet time," "daily devotion," "morning watch," or just "prayer," we all need that time in the busy run of a day when we carve out a special niche to hear from God.</u>

This is what the "simple life" is all about. The volume of noise within us must be lowered to the place where we may hear from the Master.

<u>Such a time alone with God is essential to growth, faith, nurture in Christ, character formation and service to others.</u> Solitude with the Sovereign allows for greater service to all mankind. (To show oneself, you must hide yourself, with God.)

The text of Scripture before us, Psalm 131, lifts up four principles for our pilgrimage of faith.

First, One Can Discern the Folly of *Conceit*.

David tells of a revolt in his spirit against the master of a "haughty" sense of well-being without Jehovah. Though a king, though he occupies a throne, though he receives encomiums from sycophants, though he has all the trappings of the court, he will not allow pride to push him to foolish ends.

Pride takes many forms. It can be economic exploits. It can be social standing. It can be racial rights. It can be class comfort. It can be religious righteousness. It can be political pull. It can be military muscle. No matter its stripe, pride leads to a fall!

Whatever you do, don't allow pride to shame you before God. The strongest person in the world is that person who gains strength on his/her knees before the Most High God in a daily time of meditation and "centering" so as to be useful for Him.

Conceit would tell David, and most of us, that there is sufficiency in man, especially Single Adults with all that many have today! Thus, why the need for a time of prayer. Run quickly to the job, for after all major decisions must be made; deals must close; millions hang in the balance. <u>Who has time to pray</u>?

It has been said that we suffer from "terminal busyness," and that we work under the overwhelming load of frenetic activity, without much of a product to show for the exerted effort.

For Christians, there is a sad indictment: "Busyness can be our shelter from the hard, cold fact that our relationship with Christ has become perfunctory...Our visible, external life may be laudable, but our inner spiritual life has shriveled."

Second, One Should Consider Ultimate _Concern_.

"...Nor do I involve myself in great matters, or in things too difficult for me." Such are the words of King David in this critical Psalm.

That a king would give voice to such seems preposterous, given the matters which come before him daily. Yet, we discover a man in search of a simple life. In effect, David says, "<u>What is too great for me, I leave in the hands of the Lord</u>!"

If there is to be progress in the course of daily life, the Word gives us a clear principle by which to order our private world. (Gordon MacDonald has a great book with that title.).

Matthew 6:33 reminds us who take our Christian life seriously to "seek first" the kingdom issues. This "kingdom" idea means the following:

1. Praise the Lord in all things.
2. Develop a life of discipleship.
3. Develop a Christian home, with or without a mate for life.

4. Work as a contributor to society. "If I can help some-body..."
5. Relate to family/friends.
6. Reach another with the love of God in Jesus Christ.
7. Make a difference in the world by the "<u>dash</u>" on your tombstone.

"If I can help somebody..." as I go about pursuing a "quiet" life should be our ultimate goal.

At this present moment, the "great matters" of our day are the following: AIDS, drug addiction, teen pregnancies, tax cuts, military downsizing, starvation, international strife, terrorism, hostages, national debt, nuclear weapons and more.

Anxiety results from total concern about such matters. We must take these challenges to the omnipotent One, who will handle them in His own manner.

Job, the patriarch of suffering, made the awful mistake of pondering the eternal unanswerable ("Oh, that I might find Him..."), only to later get a summons from the portals of glory to debate Jehovah, if he (Job) could answer God's "preliminary" inquiries. After his failure to do so, Job declares that God utters "things too wonderful for me."

Thus, as a Single Adult, your concern ought be to find a place, a "secret closet," wherein you may escape to unburden yourself before His majesty on high!

Third, One Should Find Soul _Composure_.

Since time alone with God reveals who God is and what He wants done, David gives a tremendous truth: "Surely I have composed and quieted my soul." David testifies concerning the merit of his time in prayer. It paid rich dividends in his soul. It put him in the right "frame of mind" beyond that of his music or food or any merriment of men.

How remarkable this assertion is because the raging storm has been stilled, the demons exorcised, the doubts faced, the hurts soothed, and the victory gained.

Develop, if you can, with the eye of faith, the picture of a man in spiritual repose, soul rest, hidden in some obscure room within an opulent palace in Jerusalem. Before departing, David has left strict orders not to be disturbed, for this is a period of quieting the soul.

Perhaps, as a crisis breaks out somewhere in the vast kingdom, someone asks, "Where is the king?," assured that he would want to be alerted in an emergency. The answer, in reply, from some court official would be, "The king is praying!" Implicit in that reply is that he must not be disturbed, for his kingship depends on his prayer posture.

To show himself before God's people, he must hide himself with God.

As a practical matter, every Single Adult should carve out ten, fifteen, thirty, sixty or more minutes from a daily schedule to meet the Lord. Beyond the specific amount of time, make it a priority to have a daily time of spiritual devotion.

Finally, We Come to *Confidence*.

There is a declared time frame for how long one can and should seek the simple life in devotion to God, as revealed in this text. "Hope in the Lord...forever."

The church, the community of faith, owes a large debt to David for this Psalm, because in it he gives a word for then, now and the age to come. To place hope in God for a lifetime would have been sufficient for most, yet we can have a "forever" confidence. Into eternity, we make our faith known by praying every day, no matter how busy or otherwise committed. It is an appointment with God! We are written into His schedule "forever."

In 1981, while a student at Southwestern Baptist Theological Seminary in pursuit of the Master's Degree, I came to greater knowledge of the value of daily devotionals. There are no words to describe the sensation of a heavenly Companion walking with me each day.

Since that time, in countless ministry settings, I have tried to call believers to such a time as David speaks of in Psalm 131, that we would all have a "quiet soul."

May I encourage you to spend the time developing this disciplined life, this simple life, this quiet life, with the promise that it will mean the world to your growth in Christ.

As a practical matter, we all need a prayer model. It should include, but not be limited to, the following:

- Adoration - Call attention to who God is
- Confession - Keep a short list of personal sins
- Thanksgiving - Recognize the Lord for His benefits
- Supplication - Let your requests be known to the Father
- Intercession - Pray for the needs of others

SELF-IMAGERY

If you really think about it, who you consider yourself and how you consider yourself is a product of something in us which we term "self image." It stems from our family of origin, culture, environment, values, and choices along the road of life.

In fact, we reflect a great deal on the self-image as we look into the invisible mirror which we set before ourselves each day. From the moment we arise, to the point we lay down, our entire day is shaped by the image we have of ourselves.

The first place we develop the self-image, of course, is the family out of which we come. We need not argue the point that what our parents and siblings do to us, with us, and before us is an important shaper of our personhood. (John Bradshaw has written about the inner child shaping the adult.)

Thus, we should recognize the importance of healthy family life. To be sure, there is a degree of what sociologists term "dysfunctionality" in every family. Yet, where there is abuse, excessive anger, criticism, unfair comparisons with other siblings, lack of opportunities, and more, the character of a child can be shaped for life.

It is true that one who comes from a network of relationships where there was criticism will learn to criticize; from love, he loves; from competition, he competes; from affirmation, he affirms; and from optimism, he is optimistic.

So far, what we should accept is that the family and the environment from which an individual emerges will play a large role in the development of the personality.

Further, we should consider the values which are conveyed, positively or negatively, along with a strong need to give young children healthy values like honesty, cleanliness, telling the truth, sharing, politeness, respect for elders, hard work, patience, fairness, love of God, love of self, love of others, responsibility, the consequences of all choices, and much more.

In so doing, we seek to influence generations.

At the same time, society's criminals, particularly young ones, have a misshapen self-image. They resort to criminal acts because somewhere there was a breakdown in the image. Their core values are missing. So, they act out aggression, say, as a means of fulfilling some prophecy of a mother or father early on. "You'll never amount to anything!"

Our aim here is to discuss the self-image as it relates to the Christian Single, not as a concrete determinative, but in order to help us cope with who we are and, more importantly, who we may become, as God yet works in our lives.

If one's self-image is poor, then, not surprisingly, one will succumb to a defeatist posture. The thought goes, from whatever background issues, "I am a nothing and I will never make a difference in this world."

At the same time, if one's self-image is healthy, the result will be a phoenixlike rise to any external challenge. This person gathers all the courage he/she can find to declare, "I can do all things through Christ who strengthens me." This is the Christian's credo in tough times. Declare it enough so that it will sustain you in the moments when your self-image is uncertain and shaky.

Furthermore, we should return to the Word of God for guidance in how one can affirm one's self-image, without being arrogant or haughty. The Song of Solomon depicts a love story between the wise king and a favored lover. According to the best research, a black maiden affirms her personhood, fully assured that she is the choicest among those Solomon loves. Although black in skin color, she is whole in her appraisal of self. She need not await the judgment of another, for she knows who she is!

Explosive, indeed, are the words of Proverbs 23:7, in that assertion, "For as he thinks within himself, so he is."

How often have we quoted such a verse without considering its relationship to a person's self-image. In fact, however, it forms the foundations for further analysis of the self-image.

Here and there in the biblical text, we run upon passages which speak implicitly about the concepts we hold about ourselves. In the Old Testament saga of Israel, as they stood at the threshold of Canaan, Moses dispatched a reconnaissance team of twelve to the Promised Land. In their assessment of the Land, ten returned and said, in Numbers 13:33, "We are grasshoppers!" What a poor self-image, for certainly God had not called them such an offensive name.

At the outset, we must affirm the placement of God's image within man as a created being. Though besmirched by sin, the "imago dei" yet remains, forming the theory of human worth. We are something because God made us! As someone remarked, "And God doesn't make junk!"

In the Creation of man, God spoke to Himself in eternity as He called a counsel in heaven. His mission would be to fashion a fascinating personage called mankind (male and female). Psalm 8:5, in its best rendering, places man a little lower than God Himself.

Therefore, our self-assessment should be shaped by an awareness of what we have within us, Who stands above us, and what we have before us.

Caution should give rise to the idea given life in Galatians 6:3, where we read, "For if anyone thinks he is something when he is nothing, he deceives himself."

The above passage teaches a lesson about conceit and haughtiness, not about the self-image, although it should keep all of us humble before the Lord.

For Single Adults, the implications are clear:

1. Since you have been made in God's image, no other person need validate your essential worth.
2. No mate, partner or companion makes you "whole," since the gift of wholeness comes from the hand of a benevolent Creator. My "better half" when speaking of

a wife or husband is faulty because we are created as "whole" persons. God has a unique form of addition in the marital scheme: 1+1=1.

3. Think and consider yourself in honesty, appraising what you have done with your life up to this moment in time. Are you a college graduate? Divorce? Single Parent? Hard Worker? Whoever you are, you can and must do the following: accentuate the positive and eliminate the negative. Shakespeare reminded us, "To thine own self be true!"

4. Seek daily to develop your highest potential spiritually, intellectually, emotionally, relationally, and financially. The late Dr. Benjamin Mays, mentor to Dr. King and other generations of men at the famed Morehouse College, challenged the students: "Low aim is the greatest sin, for anything will not do!" As a practical step, one who aspires to new levels should spend time around those who already epitomize such heights. Question: Who is your "mentor"?

5. Know most assuredly that what you possess or do not possess will never determine the real "you." Remember, you are not your home, automobile, clothes, furniture, bank account or any other "thing" of life. The patriarch Job lost all the "things" of life, but God distinguished between the "stuff" and the real Job, who despite the loss of his material possessions and family, yet maintained his personal "integrity."

6. Affirm within yourself the infinite worth you have as a child of God. As you love Him, you may love others and self. Further, every Single Adult should ponder questions such as, Where did I come from? Who am I? Why am I here? and Where am I going?

In reference to the "Who am I" issues, our world posits several possible responses:

a) Society - a number
b) School   - a grade
c) Job   - a skill; a task

d) Marriage - a partner

e) Labels   - a thing

f) Sins   - a worthless zero

In fact, when we discuss self-image, we focus on larger concepts, such as <u>origin</u>, <u>identity</u>, <u>purpose</u> and <u>goals</u>.

First, the Creation account given in Genesis refutes any illogical notion or fanciful hypothesis put forth by scientists, called the "Big Bang," or one endorsing natural selection or human evolution. Such notions leave too much to chance and randomness. We assert, in reply, that the omniscient One, God Almighty, the Ultimate Cause, brought all things (including and especially humankind) into existence. When we open the Scriptures, we find that "In the beginning God..." He is before all things came into existence. He is the Mover, for in His mind dwelt the cosmic scheme.

All ontological concepts have their terminus in God, for "in Him we live, move and exist." Thus, let it be a closed matter as to our origins. Humanity populates the sphere of planet earth because of the orderly plan and purpose of the Eternal God.

Second, the identity question can be faced squarely by knowing there is no place to venture to "find oneself." Such a search is pointless! At best, this concept emerges from a <u>psychology divorced from theology</u>.

Even in our world today, no one can find the "self" in anything secular; rather, one must begin and terminate the search in spiritual pursuits.

As never before, African Americans are listening to psychobabble, New Age cults, and other "higher conscious" movements which give forth non-sense as it pertains to the place of humanity in the ordering of life on the planet.

The horizontal aspect of our lives identifies us with others, to the extent that John Dunne was correct when he said, "No man is an island, entire of himself." When we affirm our identity, within self, we are then able to develop that identity in relation to another. The identity does not come from the other ("peer pressure"), but is stimulated by the other. Within humanity is a strong fight against isolation.

Third, our sense of purpose in life should be shaped by the knowledge that one can have any of the following: a) No purpose; b) Conflicting purposes; c) Wrong purposes; and d) A godly purpose.

Those who move about without purpose in their lives can be seen everywhere. They drift from job to job, without a grand ambition in mind. Their resume is a series of dead-end jobs. Or, in relationships, such persons fall into the same rut again and again. Aimless living means wasted potential. Without a life purpose, one is like a ship without a rudder.

On another level are those with conflicting purposes. The Scripture describes such persons as "double-minded," and expresses their frustration as "unstable in all their ways" (James 1:8). In the hustle of their existence, such persons feel pulled by conflicting impulses, and they fall prey to temptations which prevent them from attaining what they purport to really want. The friend who promises to stop by, but gets sidetracked by another promise, then never makes it, may be an example of this personality type.

A sad scenario, indeed, is the portrait of one who has an absolutely wrong purpose in life. In the main, such an individual has an ego problem. Somehow this person was convinced that life revolved around his needs, his comforts, his benefits, to the exclusion of all others. Or, one may wish to hurt others, punish others, extract revenge from others, destroy others, and more. Not surprisingly, those who have a life purpose of pleasure often die young, or sustain major injury, or face long incarceration in one of America's prisons.

But, there are those with a godly purpose in life. These individuals are not perfect. They yet fall into sin (even as they do not "wallow" there). They must get to work each day. They must balance career and family needs. They must work in various church ministries. They must do all they can to maintain a degree of sanity in a crazy world. Nevertheless, they begin each day with a desire to glorify the Master in every area and along every avenue of their conscious existence. They call on the all-sufficiency of the Lord Jesus Christ as the companion for the daily sojourn.

Each category, perhaps, calls to mind several Single Adult friends who often do not realize their need to slow down and gain a sense of life's purpose around which all thoughts should revolve.

In this regard, then, may your sense of purpose be that which glorifies the Father, allows your "light" to shine, brings others to a fuller awareness of Jesus Christ, and lasts throughout your life. In this way you will discover joy and enthusiasm for facing each new day. Dr. Myles Monroe is perhaps one of the foremost writers on the subject of "purpose." His works are highly recommended for those who seek to build self-esteem and self-worth. He gave a lecture with the following points, which are shared here for your edification:

1. To have no purpose is to accept the purpose of another.
2. The place to find purpose is the Word of God.
3. Purpose is the most critical pursuit in life.
4. Purpose for anything (even human beings) is found in the mind of the maker of it.
5. We work with God in bringing into view the purpose He has for our lives.
6. ense of purpose prevents intimidation - one cannot be turned around.
7. Many of life's failures are those who didn't know how close they were to success.

Finally, a Single person needs an over-arching idea of a goal to which he/she ultimately aspires. To be sure, such a goal must be greater than simply a home, a car, a mate or whatever. The goal must entail some way of making life better for another person.

There are two ways to view the progress of life: a "circle" or a "line."

A circle perspective means that the aspects of our existence move about in a fashion wherein we really never go
anywhere although we have much activity. Just as a circle
has no beginning and no ending, so it is with many people
among the Single Adult cohort group.

How many Single Adults move about in circular fashion: new boyfriends, new girlfriends, new clubs, new hair-
styles, new eyes, new fads/fashions, only to discover a
vicious cycle.

On the other hand, we have a linear perspective
where the person feels that there is some order and sense
to life. Since God created all things, this person knows
that intelligence yet reigns and that we are headed in a
definite direction.

As never before, we need to furnish a road map toward
an actual destination in life: wholesome fulfillment as
Singles.

The time is ripe to be the best person you can be, with
an awareness of shortcomings and hidden potential. Stop
waiting for outsiders to make you feel your worth as a person. Look into the mirror and thank God for what He has
done in creating you, exactly the way you are!

For a moment I want to share a personal story about
my growth in this area. Like many, I had a self-image problem. Yet, I was strengthened by several excellent books, as
well as the passage of time and the wisdom given by God.

In high school, I was perceived as bookish and square,
as my peers would say over and again. In fact, as a student
body leader, I was thought of as not very much fun. Also,
I was a good church boy, who attended every week, to say
nothing of speaking in many churches for various youth
programs.

Thus, I really suffered because, like all young people, I
wanted to be well thought of. Yet, my first "date" came in
the twelfth grade. I was very nervous about even asking
someone out. Eventually, thank God, I got over it!

A strange thing happened, however, after I went away

to college. In my first year there, I actually grew about 6 inches. Now, I was six feet, and I began to have a better sense of self-image. Perhaps I thought of myself as "tall, dark and handsome."

All the above means is that we all must appreciate our lives as gifts from God, and make the best of who we are. Friends may judge us by external features, yet we must accept ourselves as persons for whom Christ died.

In addition, we should seek out some biblical mentors, role models, if you will, whom we may learn from and appropriate their faith response to God. One recommended person is Daniel of the Old Testament. Daniel was that youth, then young adult, then adult, then old man, who matured (and grayed in the process) before the eyes of the astute biblical student.

Clearly, as we are reminded by Gordon MacDonald, Daniel faced various testing and challenges to his faith, but in the process of trusting God, his self-assessment increased to the point that he grew in his appropriation of truth and wisdom. His life was a sterling testament to a deeper appreciation of the role of God in the affairs of those who take Him into the boardroom, the conference room, the computer room, the judge's chambers, the doctor's office, onto the subway, into the club (OOPS!), and everywhere, so as to have a "real world faith."

Therefore, whether you are a product of a "broken" home, a Single Parent family, a "psychologically bruised" environment, a poor background or any other kind of home, recognize that the healing starts with you.

One cannot deny the fact that issues from our "past" can crop up in our "present." Much literature has been devoted to the "wounds" of childhood. We, no doubt, all cling to concepts of the "inner child" and must address the issue squarely. Healing of these emotional scars begins by recognizing that the experience of the new birth in Jesus Christ creates within us a "new creature." (2 Corinthians 5:17)

To a certain extent, these wounds must become part of

the "old things are passed away" material from our sinful, decadent past. We cannot have healthy self-images if we spend all our time rummaging through the hurts, the abuse, the wounds, the pains of the past. To the extent we rely on the Lord's empowerment, we can leave the past behind us!

Further, Romans 8:28 teaches an important life lesson: God uses "all things" in our past and present to fashion us into that which gives glory to His name.

No matter what you begin with, you can take determination, hard work, fortitude, love of God, love of others, a good attitude, a healthy ethic of the possible, mix these together, and thereby be a better person.

Somewhere along the way we have lost the sense of refinement, manners, elegance, social graces, propriety, neatness, and more. A missing word is "class."

Used here, class is not a manifestation of economics, for there are those with very little in the way of finances, yet they have "class" aplenty. We should all strive for a self-assessment which underscores the importance of dignity, personal character and integrity.

When was the last time someone remarked as to whether something said or done was carried out, "in good taste"?

Make it a priority, friend, to improve your self-image by delving deeply into the inner recesses of God, that He may show a better pathway to growth in the "inner person."

Being a Single Adult means that one must assess life in a new way, as you ponder the question of being a mate to another or a mother or father to a child. The new relationships will carry new responsibilities. Are you ready?

If you are an emotional wreck, you will simply carry that over into a relationship and, in the process, hurt others. The antidote, then, calls upon you to make the necessary alterations in thought and life.

A word to the wise: improve self and others will be attracted!

HUMAN SEXUALITY

To be human is to have a concern with issues of human sexuality, by which we mean such hotly-debated topics as Heterosexuality, Homosexuality, Bisexuality, Unisexuality, Incest, Bestiality, Masturbation, Celibacy, Abortion and more.

One treads in dangerous waters by the mere mention of these issues. It is possible to be misinterpreted. It is possible to be viewed as endorsing an idea simply by elevating it to the plane of rational evaluation. Yet, we must consider these issues, if we are to bring wholeness to the ministry to Christian Singles.

All who share in this study are presumed to have a high degree of maturity (both emotionally and spiritually), so we move on to analyze this topic by engaging in the "real world," rather than put Christian life on one side and the lives we lead in the larger society on the other. Our faith should be strong enough to allow us to take it into the "marketplace of ideas."

Our concern will be with the purpose of God, in creation, for human sexual expression, recognizing God the Creator, not psychology, not biology, not sociology, not anthropology, and not physiology, as the ultimate Voice on the subject.

At the outset, we accept as given that all persons in the Single Adult group have taken some high school or college level courses in human anatomy. This means that we can move to the step of asking some probing questions about concepts we will ultimately label as "normative" and those we will characterize as "perversions" of the created order.

In all that we discover in this study, let us remember that God loves the person, even as the actions of that person may be repugnant, or that He loves the sinner and hates the sin, or that He knows we cannot be wholly defined by what we do.

Please turn to Genesis 1--3. May we analyze God's foundational principles.

To begin at the beginning is a stroke of genius, but let's begin there because it seems like a great place to begin since we have to begin someplace!

1. *All creation begins with God, who creates (bara) out of nothing (ex-nihilo), as an exercise of His sovereign will.*

2. *The crucial verse for this study is Genesis 1:26, 27:*

   "Then God said, 'Let us make man in our image, according to our likeness; and let them rule over the fish of the sea and over the birds of the sky and over the cattle and over all the earth, and over every creeping thing that creeps on the earth.' And God created man in His own image, in the image of God He created him; male and female He created them."

   In calling together the heavenly court and anticipating the Trinity, God distinguishes the creation of man from all that comes before it. There is a "crown" to the creation of man.

   By "image" (**selem**) the Old Testament means an outward form, a copy, a duplicate, an actual, exact work. The "likeness" idea gives the notion of appearance of similarity. The image must correspond to the original. Man is created as "male and female." We have (later as names are given) Adam and Eve. The primal form of humanity shows the fellowship of man and woman. Von Rad teaches that, "God does not create man alone, neither does He create man/man or woman/woman." From the start, then, the ideal of God was for mankind to function in the mode of heterosexuality, with natural sexual expression to occur in a marital relationship of a male and a female. He even constituted the body of each to fit the other in sexual intercourse.

3. A related passage is Genesis 2:18-25, which we must work through.

Here, we discover the Lord further revealing His plan for humanity. Now, He promotes an idea of interaction with another, but the other is to be a "helper" suitable for Adam, and we are left wondering, momentarily, what or who this helper will be.

Verses 19 and 20 make it abundantly clear that the helper would not be found in the animal kingdom (this rules out bestiality!). The object of Adam's affections must be like him so as to communicate with him and have being in a similar fashion.

Still searching for the helper, God could have created another man, just like Adam, who would have been capable of rational thought and discourse (communication). According to the record here in Genesis, the Lord God turned away from the option of creating another man (this seems to rule out homosexuality!).

In a decisive, pre-ordained way, the Lord God created, using Adam's rib, someone for Adam, who was like him in thought and communication. "Eve" would be the fulfillment of Adam, mentally, emotionally, psychologically, and sexually.

The Hebrew "ish" (Adam) was united with the "ishshah" (Eve) in a mutually responsive coupling of personalities. They were created with the potential of relating to each other in a sexual way.

By verse 23, Adam is fully cognizant of the stupendous blessing he has attained from the Lord. She is that helper, that complement, that suitable one. She is now "bone of my bones, and flesh of my flesh."

In the first two chapters of the Bible, then, we encounter a creative, loving Father, who places humanity at the crowning of His creation, and mandates the male and the female, in a monogamous, heterosexual manner to be "fruitful and multiply and fill the earth" with children.

He does not create two males (a club of buddies), nor two females (a sorority of sameness), but a male and a female, for they only are able to reproduce themselves. Reproduction is part (though not all!) of what God had in mind for "normative" sexual expression in creating humanity.

The male brings the sperm and the female provides the egg in the miraculous process of human reproduction. God, of course, must sanction the relationship in marriage, if there is to be a family operating according to His blueprint.

The two sexes are quite alike, but there is a glaring difference. The man is the "male" and the woman is the "male" also. What she has special about her (aside from all the beauty, charm and grace) is the ability to carry the fetus, the baby, so she is the "fe-male."

If the Bible is our guide, from what we have discovered so far, common expressions of sexuality are struck down by the design of God: Bisexuality (preference for both sexes); unisexuality (the total loss of sexual individuality).

Bisexuality is the preference of those who wish to extend the created function of sexual expression to both male and female. In popular parlance, "AC/DC" with all that it conjures up. What we in the Christian tradition know is, such a person is deeply confused. He/she is "double-minded" and "unstable" according to the Holy Writ.

A sexual ambivalence drives such a person as he/she explores fulfillment in both males and females, seemingly, according to the mood of the moment. That we learn of such "perverse" practices among certain actors, entertainers, athletes, politicians, and other celebrities from the tabloids only worsens the situation. No matter that these persons speak openly and frankly about their proclivities, we who know the moral model as given by God must retain our ethical and moral standards.

Another preference in the wide array of practices relates to bestiality. Here, persons engage in sexual intercourse with animals, as they would with a member of the opposite sex. Most of us cannot fathom what would prompt such a person to engage in a practice that is clearly "off the screen," to say nothing of the dangerous to one's health, and, in many municipalities, illegal.

The author must confess a difficulty in rationally analyzing what can only be termed a deeply perverted lifestyle by those who favor bestiality. All that can be said is that such a person needs to turn away from this deception by Satan himself, repent, call on the Lord Jesus Christ, seek serious counseling, and begin the process of healthy emotional and sexual development.

Moreover, to be "human" is to share humanity with the opposite sex, because the animals are unfit to satisfy the God-ordained needs with the male (Genesis 2:20).

The Master designed the first male, Adam, for fulfillment with a being like himself, "fit for him," in the person of one "bone of my bones and flesh of my flesh," clearly signifying a woman.

The unity of the sexes extends to the sexual relationship and the special command to be fruitful and multiply. This is God's will. Heterosexual relationships are the only means of meeting this command.

In a world without Genesis 3, where we discover the fall of humanity, having its antecedent in the disobedience of an explicit command, we could end this treatise right now.

Since the Fall, however, we are faced with new choices, new options, new voices, all clamoring for the attention of the believer. In the cacophony of voices, I pray that we will hear God's voice, as He declares His will for our sexual expression, from His Word.

Loud, indeed, are the many voices seeking to place homosexuality before the world as an acceptable "alternative" lifestyle. We cannot dismiss the idea out of hand, but we must analyze the Word of God and then exegete the society in which we operate.

By examining the biblical references to the explosive issue of homosexuality as an alternative lifestyle, we hope that there can be understanding and guidance from God, for the practicing homosexual, as well as the wider Christian community which must minister to them.

4. *How does homosexuality differ from the design of God, as shown in several passages of Scripture?*

A. Read Genesis 19 - Sodom and Gomorrah
The key word comes in Genesis 19:5, "to know" (**yadha**) means a very pronounced sexual intimacy, normally expressed between a male and a female. The men of Sodom sought to have homosexual relations with the angels, further substantiating their reputation as "great sinners" against the Lord (Genesis 13:13).

B. Read Leviticus 18:22; 20:13 - The Holiness Code
Since God, for the nation Israel, is holy, He communicates His will through the Law, which specifically forbids male homosexual acts, for such are an "abomination."
Theologians can debate the nuances of meanings of various words, yet no one can make "abomination" even sound right, let alone, be less than a terribly serious violation of God's law.

C. Read Judges 19 - Gibeah
This passage occurs within a period when "every man did what was right in his own eyes" (Judges 21:25) and sounds strangely like the setting of today! Again, like in Sodom spoken of above, the desire is for same-sex acts, in violation of the divine order in creation. Here we have an illustration to augment the legislation.

D. Read Matthew 5:27, 28; 19:4-12 - Jesus' Position
While it is true that Jesus never speaks of homosexuality, it is also true that His statements on human sexuality defend and develop the original divine order of heterosexuality.

Another insight may relate to the fact that homosexuality was not a major problem for Palestinian Jews who kept their distance from the permissive and explorative Hellenistic culture.

E. Read Romans 1:26, 27 - Paul's Exposition
When we give up the true knowledge of God, we create substitutes and fall into diverse sins, including sexual ones. Having lost our knowledge as to Who God is, we no longer know who we are because our identity is to be found in Him.

Homosexuality (males) and lesbianism (females) are both mentioned as the exchange of "natural relations for unnatural," suggesting a willful choice, rather than a distorted disposition from birth.

This brings to light a topic in debate in many circles: is the desire for homosexual expression <u>an orientation from birth</u> or <u>learned behavior</u>.

For the Apostle Paul, these homosexual urges, impulses and acts are contrary to God's original intention and thus violate His revealed will for humanity.

F. Read 1 Corinthians 6:9 - Chaos in the Church
Paul makes the sins of sexual immorality specific by speaking of both the <u>passive</u> (**malakos** - "effeminate") and the <u>active</u> (**arsenokoites** - "Sodomite homosexual") homosexual person.

The days in which we live call for both strength in masculinity as well as grace in femininity. The preponderance of effeminate males in the church of Jesus Christ is potentially subversive to our calling as a redeemed community.

In light of the tendency to judge based on externals, perhaps our ability to witness for Christ is hampered when one visits a church only to find a majority of women, with many of the men who are there often "confused" as to their sexual orientation.

G. Read 1 Timothy 1:10 - Chaos in the Church
Paul challenges a similar problem as in Corinth above.

H. Read Jude 7 - Explanation of Judgment
In this short passage, Jude lifts up Sodom as an example of how the homosexual "went after strange flesh," and for it obtained the judgment of God.
"Strange flesh" of homosexuality must be contrasted with that of "ordained flesh" of heterosexuality within the bounds of marriage, as given by God in creation.

5. _What can we say to Single Adults who are practicing homosexuals (male and female), yet who want to accept Jesus Christ as Savior?_

A. The practice must stop! To go on with acts which are clearly in violation with God's will risks severe judgment. At the same time, one must understand that there are probably pleasures involved which make it difficult to stop. Sin has an element of pleasure and fun, although the pleasure is passing.

B. Repentance is the next step as you ask God's forgiveness. The whole idea of repentance is a change in attitude, away from your will (to be a homosexual), to a godly will (heterosexual fulfillment). Read Acts 2:38.

C. Get involved in a church fellowship that affirms you as a person made in the image of a loving God, who gives a higher pattern for your life.

D. Recognize the potential of God to convert and conform you to the new standard of Christ in you "the hope of glory."
Read 1 Corinthians 6:11. Some of the believers at Corinth had been "washed," "sanctified," and "justified" in the name of Christ!
There is abundant hope - even for you! Trust Him and accept it!

E. <u>In light of the spread of AIDS, please see a doctor</u>. Those who have a background of homosexuality may unwittingly spread the virus via sexual intercourse. Every new partner one takes on, in unprotected sex, is vulnerable to this disease, which, at present, has no known cure. More and more, AIDS is spread through ignorance. Too many are dying from this scourge without knowledge. When sexual practices become life-threatening, the Christian Church must speak up, with a loving, caring and redemptive word.

In the United States, 400,000 people have contracted AIDS since 1981, and 250,000 people have died from it. Such grim statistics make AIDS a subject for future study and discussion within the Christian Singles ministry.

F. <u>Remain positive as you grow into a new way of life. Growth in faith is not instantaneous. It takes time and effort. It will be worth whatever you must go through in order to reach the intention of God in creating you</u>.

6. A final word for this debate.

Perhaps it is too strong to conclude with some that the dreaded and deadly AIDS virus is God's penalty against homosexuals, especially because drug users, persons receiving tainted blood and babies have been exposed.

On the other hand, every person must ask a deep question of moral responsibility for "doing my own thing," when this "thing" is in direct violation of the revealed will of God.

Lost in this discussion is the inescapable anatomical crudity of homosexuals "making an <u>entrance</u> where God made an <u>exit</u>"!

The act and inclination are both biologically backward, anatomically abnormal, physiologically perverse, and theologically treacherous.

Even after the above, we must challenge the Christian Church to sound a "certain" tone on this subject. The fall of Rome and other great centers, throughout history, has stemmed from their tolerance of homosexuality. We have a biblical foundation upon which to base our opposition to the practice.

What is particularly troubling, as proponents of heterosexuality seek to hold up the God-ordained ideal, is the tendency of state legislatures, gay advocacy groups, the media, and others to thwart such efforts by painting the homosexual "perversion" as comparable to God's design. Public opinion polls must not determine what is the standard of righteousness. Laws may be changed to allow for homosexuals to adopt children, say, but this will not make same-sex partnering right in the sight of God!

Even as many practicing homosexuals "come out of the closet," we must sound the alarm that such a practice intentionally deviates from the divine ideal.

For those who feel as if the Church unnecessarily "picks" on homosexuals, or makes it the "big sin," let me remind you that practitioners of this sin (as defined by the Word), in actuality, make themselves the target by demanding civil rights, by marching in parades, by "coming out," and in other ways. If anything, by their boldness, such persons "pick" themselves out!

(Adulterers don't parade down the street, asking that they be affirmed in their sinful acts. Why not? Because they are, rightly, ashamed and seek not to be discovered. But, our gay brothers and sisters are arrogant and exhibitionist in their sin. Therefore, we must allow the Bible to be heard on their acts. Where the Word allows the Church to speak, it must! Homosexuality is a sin before God!)

Another concern in the area of human sexuality which we must consider, in the interests of thoroughness, relates to masturbation. It is quite controversial. It has a taboo attached. In the 90s, the mere mention of the subject by the Surgeon General, a black woman, Dr. Jocelyn Elders, was enough to get her fired from a lofty position.

What do we make of the subject of "self-pleasure"?

According to surveys, about 60 percent of adult men and 40 percent of adult women engaged in masturbation in the last year. Add to this, the number of shops which cater to those wishing to purchase sexual aid devices. Further, there is anecdotal evidence that the practice is quite pervasive.

There is a text of Scripture, Genesis 38:9, which many have taken as a proscription against masturbation. Here, Onan, does what is termed, "spilled his seed on the ground." From that passage, many warn that such a practice is forbidden. Close examination of that text reveals, however, that another act, "coitus interruptus" may have been occurring, as a means of preventing an unwanted pregnancy. This, in fact, was a very early example of positive birth control.

If we forbid masturbation, it must be on other grounds. We should consider again the fact that God made sexual function a part of our makeup, to be indulged in within the sanctity of marriage, for procreation and pleasure. Any sexual expression outside marriage goes against the biblical teaching.

Masturbation raises problems because the pleasure one gives to self is outside the biblically acceptable realm. Sex is to be between heterosexuals in a monogamous, marital relationship.

With the Bible clear on the possibilities of sexual fulfillment, the sincere Christian Single, therefore, is presented with the option of celibacy, or intentionally refraining from sexual activity. The question is, "Can all Singles practice celibacy?" "If so, for how long?"

The two most debated passages relating to celibacy are what Jesus taught in Matthew 19 and what the Apostle Paul declared in 1 Corinthians 7. Biblical scholars and commentators have argued these texts to fit many preconceived notions.

What makes the matter all the more problematic is that Matthew 19 must be properly exegeted in light of the situation of that day. In addition, 1 Corinthians is part of a written correspondence, only part of which we have to examine (Paul's two letters, but not their letters). After all is said, however, many yet seek clarity on the subject.

In Matthew 19, in response to the disciples comment, "...it is better not to marry," the Lord Jesus spoke on the subject of celibacy. He then launched into a discussion of this most important of issue.

"Not all men can accept this statement, but only those to whom it has been given. For there are eunuchs who were born that way from their mother's womb; and there are eunuchs who were made eunuchs by men; and there are also eunuchs who made themselves eunuchs for the sake of the kingdom of heaven. He who is able to accept this, let him accept it."

Clearly, celibacy is not available to all Christian Singles. The Lord Himself makes this plain, for it is a spiritual gift from God to certain persons. He explains three types of "eunuchs": 1) those physically unable; 2 those socially disinclined; and 3) those spiritually minded.

Within each category there are persons who live healthy and productive lives, without a concern for their manner of sexual expression. The issue has been settled. They are able to concentrate on other pursuits. Among this grouping, most prominently, would be priests and nuns, along with others who live out their lives in a wide array of occupations and callings.

When one has the spiritual gift of celibacy, the sexual aspect of one's being will be regulated by a greater sense of well-being in one's career, one's ministry, one's relations (platonic) with friends and others. Moreover, God will, through His Word, the insight of the Holy Spirit, and an inner peace, make it known that one so inclined is, in that non-act, giving glory to His name.

LOOKING IN THE MIRROR

ME
?

Unless one is overwhelmed by self (narcissistic), all of us pause when approaching a mirror, for it reveals to us more of us and more about us than we care to know. It reveals pimples, warts, scratches, scabs, unhealed places, sores, bruises, bumps and more. (Thank God we stopped at the face in the mirror!) But, when we seek improvement, the only effective means is to begin with a thorough examination of the area to be covered. We must face the "self" in order to improve it.

When we view our reflection in the mirror, it allows us to take the necessary steps toward improvement in the interior space. The mirror is without value if one remains in the same position. Mirrors only aid those who take a gander in order to correct what they see. For some Christian Singles, other persons have seen our defects, but they, perhaps trying to be kind, have not alerted us to the need for growth. When we ourselves peer into the glass, may we not fear the reflection staring back at us.

The physical mirror is but one of the many we must peer into, if there is to be growth and development. Also, we should consider the mental one, for the mind must be fed like any other live organism. It should feed on matter that increases the likelihood of further expansion. What goes into the mind will determine the direction one takes in life. There should be a continuing thirst for knowledge, for information, for wisdom, for experiences which will stretch the human potential. This mirror allows one to make a healthy comparison with others of similar age and background.

Another mirror we can peer into is that of the career model. One should not settle for "any job that pays" because we spend so much of the "self" at the work place. Thus, it should fit into a larger plan and purpose for us. We are not robots, so some of what we do on the job should reflect what we are suited to do in life. Simply put, the most fulfilled person is the one who, if economically feasible, would perform his/her tasks without compensation, for the sheer thrill of doing what one is perfectly suited to do. The challenge is to discover that job where one gets up in the morning eager to arrive and leaves at the end of the day regretful for quitting time.

Further still, there is an <u>emotional</u> mirror. This is quite personal, for it calls for maturity, as the emotional makeup of many lags behind their corresponding chronological point. In other words, too many Christian Singles are emotionally immature. (Some relationships are imperiled by the fact that a tall boy or a tall girl is masquerading as adults!). One of the first lessons of maturity is that life does not owe anyone anything. A spoiled child expects life to cater to all his/her whims. We who know the realities also know that life is unfair, institutional racism exists, conditions are stacked against the kindly, and nice folks sometimes finish last! Nevertheless, we press on, in faith, with a dogged determination to succeed no matter the price.

A forgotten mirror for many is the <u>ethno-cultural one</u>. We need to affirm anew our blackness. This may take the form of Afrocentrism in dress (Kente cloth), in hairstyle (cornrows), in language (adopt new names), in customs (Kwanzaa celebrations), and more. We must awaken the dormant pride within which will teach African Americans the power of the black dollar, trading with one another, buying where we have a "stake" in the economy, and trusting our own kin and kind. We need not emulate the cultural traditions of others, for we have a vibrant and rich history and heritage, for which we can be proud. Africa should take on greater significance in our concerns as a homeland. Its rich resources should call us back again and again. If we choose to do the work, the American mosaic will be improved by our ebony presence.

The greatest mirror of all, however, is the <u>spiritual</u> one, for it undergirds all we see in the other mirrors. Without the foundation of faith in God, manifested in a daily relationship with the Savior Jesus Christ, given life in the indwelling Holy Spirit, we may have many possessions, but life will be empty, pointless and wasted. Again, I challenge some person to really find what God wants from you. When you discover the purpose of His creation, then you will soar in the Spirit.

To look in the mirror, one should have a reason. Perhaps to check the makeup, or to determine if all hair is in place, or to notice any potentially embarrassing spots or stains, or to insure that you make the best presentation possible to the world (one never gets a second chance to make a first impression).

As it turns out, the mirror we speak of is the mirror of the "self." All we desire is personal growth. The question turns at the point of, how do we attain it?

1. Appropriate a spirit of gratitude to God, each day, for the bounty of health, strength, favor and grace. Proverbs 3 teaches, "In all thy ways acknowledge him, and he shall direct thy path."

    Too many people have built elaborate residences on the narrow cull de sac called "Complaint Way," rather than the far broader "Thank You" Boulevard. Hallelujah!

    When you consider the brevity of our existence, some of the things we get excited over (home, car, clothes, cash, conveniences, credit cards, and more) lose their importance when weighed against good health and a loving family.

2. Pray for a vital relationship with God, who loves each of us as we are, yet He seeks to develop in us new attitudes, new faith, new conviction, new insight, and new responsiveness to His prompting to significant service to Him, in the lives of others.

    "Let your light so shine before men...that they may

glorify the Father in heaven" (Matthew 5).

The body of Christ (of which every believer is a critical part) carries forth the agenda of God at this present juncture in human history. Question: "Are you a participator or spectator?"

3. Avoid critical and judgmental positions relative to self and others. Negativism eats away at the core of our being, like cancerous cells, and should thus be avoided, if one is to make progress. While "misery loves company," the miserable, critical will not long have "company," for no one likes to be around sour folks!

"And why do you look at the speck that is in your brother's eye, but do not notice the log that is in your own eye?" (Matthew 7:3). Too many people abhor the evil in others while condoning the same imperfections in self.

4. Actively seek the good in others and help them to pursue it.

When we get away from a life preoccupied by our own aggrandizement, and advancement, we can then appreciate the strivings of another. Find someone (usually a friend) to help with their goals, and, in the process, in a reciprocal fashion, the law of "sewing" and "reaping" will show a positive outcome for you.

5. Learn the principles of optimism. See the glass as half-full rather than half-empty.

If it is true that, "what you see is what you get," then shouldn't this tell us to look for the best, the most positive, most affirming, more uplifting spin on all events? The death of civilization will come when cynicism and a jaded spirit overtake us, as no one expects anything but the worst. As a Christian Single, there is a tendency to assess your station in life, principally as you have no mate, and derive from that a cynicism towards others who were once in the same life condition.

6. Continually seek for new books, interesting articles, novel hobbies, creative adventures, and new friendships, so

as to add "spice" and "variety" to the mundane and the routine.

The mirror you peer into should convince you that it has seen the old for too long. Change is good. Change is, however, scary, for it takes us into the region of the unknown and the unfamiliar. Yet, even if it is as simple as learning to ski, ride a horse, fence, calligraphy, a foreign language, or something else, do it. Break the cycle of the rote, the monotonous.

(Hint: When you engage in new experiences, you may improve your chances of meeting a potential life partner, husband, wife, or significant other.)

7. Study the Word for its application to your life. Ask the Spirit of God to breathe life into passages you have read and re-read over the years for a daily sense of direction. Along the way, we come to realize that the Bible is not a book to read for general reading, but rather it calls for action.

Is there a new truth to discover? A bad habit to break? A difficult relationship to sever? A bold challenge to face? A debt you owe? A situation to deal with? A resolution to adopt? A promise to hold to? A God to call on? A Savior to claim? A Presence to confide in?

8. Evaluate your present position against an overall life plan, to determine, accurately, the extent to which you are making progress or simply "marking time."

The Apostle was on target when he said, "I press toward the mark for the prize of the upward call of God in Jesus Christ" (Philippians 3:14). He foreshadowed the hymn writer who called us to "Higher Ground."

9. Check your spending patterns against the standard of necessity. Have you gotten caught in the clutches of this acquisitive culture? Oscar Wilde commented, "We know the price of all things, and the value of nothing!"

Do you spend money you don't have, on things you don't need, trying to impress people you don't like, all for the thrill that won't last?

10. Examine the company you keep and the role of all "friends" in your life.

Are you better or worse off because of your closest friends? Do such persons confirm you in your fantasies, or do they confront you in reality? (Another chapter will address friendship in a more detailed fashion.).

11. Find something big, something important and thrust yourself, headlong, into it, even as you know that it will outlive you. The homeless shelter, the AIDS hospice, the senior citizen's facility, the day care, the political campaign, the prison ministry, the food pantry, the illiteracy program, the tutorial ministry, the blood drive, the voter registration effort, the Big Brothers, the Big Sisters, or dozens of other important works.

The metaphorical mirror we have constructed should remind us that we must make an investment in some noble, grand, and worthy act, so as to validate our stay here on the planet. Some wise person has asserted that, "Service is the rent we pay for the space we occupy."

12. Steer away from a preoccupation with self-pity, no matter what your circumstances, for you may not realize how many would love to be in your place.

One of the most enduring, captivating movies ever made is entitled, *It's A Wonderful Life.* Each year around Christmas it is shown. The premise is that a man loses a great deal of money belonging to others. He feels as if his life were a mistake. He attempts suicide. He is saved by an angel, who takes the bewildered man up on his wish that he'd never been born. The angel shows the man what life would have been like had he not been born. By the movie's end, the distraught man learns that "life is good" because his family and his friends show forth unstinting love, forgiveness and compassion. He then learns to thank God for all things. Even in a jaded, cynical world, that movie still resonates in the human heart.

INTERPERSONAL RELATIONSHIPS

Friendship describes the person whom one knows well, for whom there is an affinity, who shares an emotional tie, and stands on the same side in life's journey. There is a tremendous amount of good will between the two. Barriers are broken down, the conversation moves smoothly, the references are familiar, and the trust is strong. For most people, it is a valuable concern.

We are bound together in a cord of human concern, one for the other. Since the dawning of time, ours has been a trek through life in search of those with similar interests as our own.

Terry McMillan's book, "Waiting to Exhale," gives a glimpse into the role friendship plays by chronicling the lives and loves of four African American women of the '90s. At times, this book is hilarious, poignant, frightening, and insightful, as it portrays the resiliency of friendship amid the ups and downs of the dating years. What we find in it helps us move further in an analysis of friendship.

How do you choose friends? With whom do you spend your free time? If you were to find yourself stranded on a desert island, who would you want there with you? If you had only a few weeks to live, with whom would you want to spend this precious time? How did you meet this person? How does he/she make you feel? What does he/she bring out in you? How would your life be different without such a person?

In order to understand interpersonal relationships, it would be to our advantage to pursue concrete answers to the above inquiries.

When one begins to explore such questions, one must go back in thought to the initial meeting with the most intimate of friends. Often, it occurred in the context of a social or career-related gathering. Someone probably provided the introductions, a conversation ensued, some laughter (or controversy) developed, one or both sensed a "connection" of minds, time went on, cards or phone numbers were exchanged, a call was made, another meeting took place, more conversation, and the friendship blossomed.

Such a scenario occurs, no doubt, hundreds of times, but most persons remain to us only "acquaintances," rather than the more meaningful "friends." What moves a person from the former into the latter category?

What is the Value of Friends?

Friends, first of all, make life fun and fulfilling, while sharing a portion of their outlook on life, as well as listening to us flesh out who we are in important times of sharing. Often when we look through photo albums, we come across friends who were "there" at pivotal and important moments in our life journey. Maybe it was an anniversary, a birthday, a funeral, a new promotion, a special day when we felt that special bond with another.

In the biblical story of the downfall of Job, in the early episodes, the Scripture tells us that his three friends heard of his adversity, came to him, and sought to sympathize with him. They wept with their friend, for they recognized the depths of his pain. Over the course of seven days and nights they sat with him, in silence, as they practiced the ministry of "presence." One could say that they did more in "just being there" than when they tried to determine the reason for Job's suffering. In this example, perhaps we may learn that what friends need in time of crisis is our presence!

At the same time, friends allow us to make mistakes

without adopting a judgmental posture or looking at us as a "loser," a "jerk," a "bum," or some other derisive way of viewing oneself. They affirm us as having worth and purpose. If they must pull us out of a "funk," a true friend will be right over! This is critical because we need a network of persons who are able to zero in on the hurting place and apply the balm of kindness.

There are times, however, when the best a friend can do for us is to confront us, challenge us, tell us what no one else will. Some addict or drug abuser needs a friend to call a halt to a ruinous lifestyle. Even as one may resist it initially, we have a moral obligation to call a friend to accountability in a particular area. We should, in fact, grant to the true friend(s) the right and the responsibility to do such, if we want to improve. The wise friend exercises tact, timing, love and patience when thus engaged.

Friends also make themselves available and accessible during the tragedies of life, along with those rare, infrequent triumphs of life; these special persons help to maintain our psychological equilibrium. Often, they will not wait to be called upon, but they have a way of lovingly "taking over" when the need arises in our lives.

Further, friends give us a sense of normalcy in the vicissitudes of our fragile existence; they let us know that there is order in life. After we rant and rave about the unfairness of it all, they provide the calming influence we need to face the situation. This is the "sounding board" person who listens patiently to all sorts of scatter-brain ideas then says, "Now will that work?"

These "significant others" (to borrow a term from sociology) are quite important in the scheme of our life plan. Therefore, we should affirm friends and hold them close to our hearts. We may not have a multitude of friends, because the true ones are quite rare, but if you have one, consider yourself blessed by God. As we mature, more of us recognize the value of long-term, tried-and-true friends.

How should one choose a friend?

1. Find a good listener, because such a person will need to "be there" for you (and vice versa).
2. Look for someone who has similar life interests: sports, health, career, spiritual life, humor and more.
3. Try to spend time in unstructured activities. The "real" person comes out during such periods.
4. Be a bit selfish: consider how that other person will benefit you, rather than take from you (Be this way as well).
5. Ask yourself can you dream together about the future, with a plan that you will value one another despite successes for either party.
6. Make it a point to gain objectivity within a friendship because only a true friend can say, "You're wrong!" If you have someone like this, hold on to that friend, for he/she is true.

What does the Bible teach about friendship?

Proverbs 17:17 - "A friend loves at all times, and kinsfolk are born to share a brother is born for adversity."

Proverbs 18:24 - "A man of many friends comes to ruin, but there is a friend who sticks closer than a brother."

Proverbs 27:6, 17 - "Faithful are the wounds of a friend...Iron sharpens iron, so one man sharpens another."

John 15:13-15 - "Greater love has no one than this, he one lay down his life for his friends. You are my friends, if you do what I command...."

James 2:23 - "...And Abraham believed God...and he was called the friend of God."

As the Bible gives many principles, as we discover in the passages cited above, it shines the brightest light when it describes, in narrative form, true, godly, positive, affirming friendship in a concrete life experience, such as the friendship of David and Jonathan.

In 1 Samuel chapters 18-20 a rich story unfolds of manly love, without any pretense, between the king's son

(Jonathan) and God's heir apparent (David). Over the course of some time, their souls were "knit together," indicative of the enduring nature of their friendship. It was a giving relationship, a growing relationship, and a strong relationship. Jonathan's jealous father Saul could not fathom how his son would favor David and protect David, even from his evil machinations. The friendship helps us understand that God can give all of us a true friend for the life journey. When you read the story, you will see first-hand that a friend is a rare commodity, worthy of special protection, and the source of thanksgiving to God for making it possible in the first place. As word reached David of Jonathan's death, the would-be king was moved to deliver a moving eulogy, the likes of which few can compare: "I am distressed for you, my brother Jonathan; you have been very pleasant to me. Your love to me was more wonderful than the love of women. How the mighty have fallen."

There was nothing effeminate about their love one for the other. It was manly. They no doubt could hug one another as men. They both loved women, but they found a commonality in their friendship. They could and did protect one another. They loved each other unselfishly, thereby providing a context for viewing friendship even in our day.

Few relationships today reach that level because we fear the misinterpretations of the relationship, or have insecurities about our impulses, but what these men shared was quite precious. We should aspire to such a level of brotherly and sisterly intimacy.

In the end, of course, the best way to have a friend is to be a friend. Go the extra mile for another. Be exactly the kind of friend you seek.

As an exercise, you may want to write down the names of your closest friends. Take the moment to thank God for ushering them, above other acquaintances, into the innermost chambers of your heart and mind. Take the extra step of expressing by word or deed the appreciation you have for them.

FOUNDATIONS FOR MARRIAGE

Any two persons with a sincere faith in the Lord Jesus Christ, contemplating marriage, should take these steps in a very serious manner. As the standard marital vows declare, "it is not by any to be entered into unadvisibly or lightly; but reverently, discreetly, advisedly, and in the fear of God."

This means that there should be a serious appraisal of what one may be getting into. We need, therefore, to begin with an understanding of ourselves, individually, then move to understand the nature of the commitment under consideration. We should work at the foundation level before we attempt to construct a happy marriage and a healthy home life.

At the foundation level, we will learn about the concept of God for healthy sexual expression and the development of the family. This could be an exhaustive study in itself, yet we will briefly consider the biblical witness as it relates to the family. (There are books listed in the Bibliography at the back which will serve to supplement this material for those who need to read further. In the interest of brevity, some material has been condensed. Most important, in addition, is that one take advantage of pre-marital counseling, in an extensive format, by one's pastor or staff minister prior to setting the date for marriage.)

That the Bible begins with the creation of humankind proves that God takes a keen interest in the family as the bulwark of society. He institutes the family as the most important spiritual grouping for the transmission of values and the formation of the human character. The family has a special blessing attached to it, for it will be the means of peopling the earth and propagating the species.

The family is, therefore, a spiritual institution before it

is a social one. In our modernity, as we turn from spiritual truth, we tend to forget what God had in mind in constructing the initial family, headed by Adam. Yet we are not left without understanding: "For this cause a man shall leave his father and mother and shall cleave to his wife; and they shall become one flesh" (Genesis 2:24).

We gather, then, that the family unit is to be protected and preserved, at all costs, and beyond our capacity to comprehend the nature of the commitment. The spiritual dimension of the marital relationship means that there are, in actuality, three participants in the relationship: God, the man, and the woman.

The social aspect of the family helps us grasp how the society benefits from healthy homes and strong families. Long tomes have been devoted to how crime diminishes, and other social maladies are prevented where there are intact families. We can understand the importance of this as so many juvenile delinquents emerge from so-called "broken homes" and "fractured families."

Stability in society develops where there are families insistent on sharing the traditional values of a culture, which they themselves have gained from parents, going back many generations. We must fight for the preservation of family life. Every would-be couple is responsible for the maintenance of stable families. Each marital breakdown contributes to the larger breakdown of the moral order.

What, then, should one consider in preparation for marriage?

The young disciples listened with rapt attention as their leader spoke of the exacting standards of matrimonial commitment as originally designed by God. When He concluded, they reasoned that, by virtue of His high view of marriage and low view of divorce, the best alternative would be to remain in the Single Adult population.

Yet, with the jarring suddenness of a "slammed door," they were told that even perpetual singleness was only possible by a special gift ("eunuch" in that day, "celibacy" in ours) of the Lord.

Matthew 19 records this thrilling discussion between Jesus Christ and His apostles. It serves as a fitting point of departure for a fuller analysis of the foundations of Christian marriage. We should be concerned with why God conceived and ordained marriage initially.

Is marriage for freedom or confinement? Happiness? Punishment? Joy? Pain? Child-bearing? Companionship?

Our concepts of marriage must be purged of the diverging and potentially damaging views we bring to it, from soap operas, popular culture, movies, music, secular books, television, what-we-saw-our-folks-do, and more. Most of us have notions that do not square with the Word, and, not surprisingly, we feel let down when a relationship does not equate with the initial concept or the rosy scenario.

In the soap opera (I know you don't watch them!), there is a never-ending cycle of spin-off relationships, with adultery rampant, and several second, third, and fourth marriages. Add to this the fathering of children in a haphazard fashion. Lost in all of this is the damage done to the psyche as too many expect their romances to reach the Hollywood-produced version. The result is a hopeless fantasy.

The popular culture contributes to the distorted view of marriage by the movies and music which fill the eye and ear, with excursions into the dream world. Two people "meet" across a crowded room, establish strong eye contact, engage in perfect conversation, send forth "vibes" of attraction, agree or disagree for subsequent encounters, fall madly in love, have terrific sex, run into a small problem, resolve it, dress perfectly, work tirelessly, and live happily ever after; all in the space of 90 minutes. Most times, there is a musical accompaniment, which swells at just the right moment. If you prefer the radio, you hear just the right words to sweep a person off her feet. But, such is not reality!

Of late, many self-help books have come into print, with the implicit promise to teach you all you need to know about a man's needs, his yearnings, how to please him sexually, how to make him pop the question and more. Also, these books purport to teach you how to tap into her insecurities, give her ultimate pleasure, appeal to her sensitivities, and know when she attempts to force a commitment. What happens, in the main, is that readers learn to perpetuate the "game" that all who date hate so much. Again, we miss reality.

On the other hand, there are those who take their cues from the ideal of their parent's relationship (or lack thereof). Such persons reason, "I will be just like Mother. I will emulate her ways. I will carry myself as she did." Or, a man may say, "Dad was the best provider. He was always there for us. He and Mom never had a problem. He always knew what to do. I'll follow his lead." This method of preparing for marriage, however plausible it may seem, is also inadequate, because many persons have an idealized, romanticized version of their parents' relationship. Also, for the most part, our parents were from another generation, one whose world view was much less complex relative to roles and expectations. In their day, men worked, women stayed home, cooked, cared for the children, and kept hearth and home. Theirs was a less cynical time, for all the institutions were not under attack, as is the case today. Also, today we have two-career families, high incomes, throwaway, shallow commitments, heavy debt, with new, ill-defined roles for each partner. In such a state, marriages crumble.

An older man was engaged in conversation with a younger man. The topic turned to the uncertain state of the younger man's marriage. He asked his senior friend, "Why is it so hard?" The older gentleman replied, "Your generation expects so much and receives so little; my generation expected so little, but gained so much." (Truer words were never spoken!)

What, then, should form the foundation of our concept for marriage?

The following gives the definitive word of Jesus Christ, God in the flesh, relative to marriage, the deepest physical and spiritual unity for humanity:

"And He answered and said, Have you not read, that He who created them from the beginning made them male and female, and said, 'For this cause a man shall leave his father and mother, and shall cleave to his wife; and the two shall become one flesh'? Consequently they are no longer two, but one flesh. What therefore God has joined together, let no man separate."

Whatever else we say about marriage, we must at least hear these authoritative words, falling from the lips of One "who knows more about living than anyone who has ever lived." Christ furnishes the absolute foundation for marriage.

The ideal given by Jesus Christ places God firmly in the center of the marital relationship, for, from the "beginning," God's original intent was to build the society around the family unit, as He made us as male and female, spiritual, social and sexual beings.

The relationship, as intended by the Master, was to be monogamous, exclusive, and greater than any other human relationship. It would involve a "leaving" and a "cleaving" on the part of both parties, so as to ensure that the other felt fully affirmed in the new unit of life and love.

There was also to be a process of oneness, for we underscore the words, "shall become" one flesh. It will not occur instantaneously, not on the wedding day, not immediately after saying, "I do," but at some later point, provided each remembers the Lord in the daily development of the commitment.

Finally, He teaches us that the relationship is to be permanent, for no one is to put it "asunder." This proscription has formed the basis for the Christian in his/her abhorrence of divorce. God meant, from the earliest conceptualizing of the family, that the relationship would be inviolate.

Let us turn, briefly, to a practical consideration as to what drives persons to pursue marriage in our day.

H. Norman Wright, noted author of "So You're Getting Married," as well as a Christian family counselor, writes that people marry for at least the following ten major reasons:

1. To be taken care of by a mate.
2. Pre-marital pregnancy.
3. Rebound from a previous relationship.
4. Rebellion (among the young) against authority.
5. Loneliness as a Single Adult.
6. Escape from a negative home environment.
7. Strong physical attraction.
8. Social pressure from family and peers.
9. Guilt and pity for perspective mate.
10. Physical and emotional need fulfillment.

While there may be some important rationales in the list above, I believe that all are inadequate bases for making such a life-long commitment of one's life.

There must be higher purposes, higher aspirations, higher aims, or else one should remain as a Single Adult.

"So, why do you want to get married?"

In a further development of his thesis, Wright gives seven needs from the Scripture that should undergird marriage.

First, There is *Completion*. Please read Genesis 2:18, 24.

Completion means that fellowship and friendship are involved, as both share beliefs and dreams about the future. In the process, each finds a deep, mature need to spend all of life with the other. This concept of completion should not be taken to mean that one is "half" in search of the "better half," for God works with whole persons, if the relationship is to be healthy.

Second, We See _Consolation_. Please refer to Genesis 2:18.

Most important here is the fact that all animals were brought to Adam, yet "for Adam there was not found a helper suitable for him." This lack, then, causes God to make a special creature for Adam, from Adam, whom he called Eve. Being thoroughly consoled Adam said, "<u>Wooooo - man</u>!"

Adam got excited because God gave him exactly what he needed in a mate. She would complement him, and he would do the same for her. There would be a uniting in one another.

Third, We Discern _Communication_. Please read Genesis 2:3.

Since talking involves a degree of exposure of oneself, in marriage, the couple who spends much time in communication and conversation develops an intimacy they would never have otherwise.

(Parenthetically, if Adam and Eve had discussed the words of Satan, would they have fallen to his whims? Just something to think about.)

Fourth, There Is _Coition_. Please refer 1 Corinthians 7:4-5.

This word relates to sexual fulfillment or the pleasure principle within the bounds of holy, committed, marital love. Sexuality is the celebration of God's continuing creativity. Several Christian authors speak of the need for a life of sexual sharing.

Here the emphasis is placed on intimacy and emotional intercourse. As Paul teaches, this sharing prevents Satan from gaining a point of temptation. Also, consider the words of Hebrews 13:4.

Fifth, We Discover _Creation_. Please read Genesis 1:28.

Within the marital state, the couple has the blessed privilege of bringing another person into the world, by a conscious act, thereby obeying God's command to "be fruitful and multiply." History, heritage and hope can be handed to new and succeeding generations.

Sixth, We Come to _Correlation_. Please refer to Ephesians 5:21-33.

Since the Christian home is crucial to God, because it resembles a microcosm of the Body of Christ, and because God chooses to speak of the Church as His "bride," the family should be the church in miniature.

Finally, We Find Chri_stianization_.

A stable, loving Christian family has the potential for being a major evangelistic force on earth. There is something of the strength of the family for the spread of morals, decency and values.

This brief overview should serve to strengthen the foundation for the consideration of marriage in a mature manner. It has not been exhaustive, as there are many excellent Christian books, tape series, workshops, counseling sessions, videos and more to help the eager student.

A final word: please do not rush into marriage without spending quality time in prayer, well before you ask for or accept a marital commitment. Please take the Lord's guidance, and wait for Him to give a clear, definite answer to your inquiry. There are lasting repercussions to a hasty decision. It is better that one remain Single, than to move into the murky, uncertain waters with the wrong person.

In short, think long and hard on exactly what you may be getting into. The wise person thinks, "<u>Look before you leap; you might be getting into something deep!</u>"

There should be no rush in moving toward marriage, for those who seek a strong, stable one. In preparing oneself, spiritually, emotionally, psychologically, economically, and socially, the emphasis should be on asking oneself, and other mature saints, the questions necessary to guide wise decision-making.

For example, when preparing for marriage, realize that "everything" changes in your life!

You are about to have someone to whom you are accountable, in your time, your spending, your sexual relations, your goings/comings, and much more. If you have lived as a Single person for any length of time, being used to a sense of freedom, to some degree this new commitment will mean a lifetime adjustment, which at first will be a major disorienting of your routines.

Further, your spiritual life will now entail how you respond to God, love Him, and grow in Him, with the added consideration of growth in your marriage. (For this reason, persons marrying unbelievers, persons of other religious persuasions, and even different denominations may develop problems.) This should be a critical concern when you entertain thoughts of marriage.

Psychologically, ask yourself if you are really ready to take on a mate, or is it simply a projection of fantasy from when you were a little boy or girl. Think of it, in marriage you become a part of another, forever, with major consequences in your appraisal of the world beyond.

There is also the economic consideration when marriage is mentioned. We should not dismiss this concern, due to the role finances (or the lack thereof) play in the death of many marriages. The best advice is to put your finances in order. Devise a budget and stay with it. Ask yourself how it would be when you have to try to pay bills with another; how do you bring all the separate credit cards/credit histories together; how do you bring two apartments/two condos, etc. together into one new home; what do you do with all the separate furniture/appliances/dishes, etc. These issues are not trivial. You must have practicality in marriage preparation.

In this regard, some discuss a "pre-nuptial" agreement, as many Singles have rather substantial real estate and stock/bond holdings. When one's portfolio is large, this concern is not inconsequential. No matter your financial position, recognize that some adjustments will come with a marriage. As an individual, prior to the wedding, you should think through this and related topics, with financial planners, if possible, and with your prospective mate.

MATE SELECTION

While all persons need not actively pursue a marital relationship, for those who do, we need to consider the matter in a serious fashion. In the 1990s, I am mindful of the supposed new-found contentment which operates under the guise, "<u>I'm not looking for anybody</u>." What drives such a position is the theory that, if one looks, then one will not find; so, just wait for it to happen, and you save the headache.

Such a position borders on fatalism and resignation. The believer in Jesus Christ is not one who accepts the "whatever" in life, for we can and should bring our "requests" before the throne of God. We should learn that we may ask, even if God is not predisposed to grant a particular prayer petition. Just leave it with Him, even if you ask for the wrong thing. Be daring in your Christian walk. "Nothing ventured, nothing gained!"

In many quarters, this hypocritical stance even attempts to cloak itself in piety: "<u>I'm just waiting for the Lord. Whatever He has for me or does not have for me is all right</u>!" But, the Word plainly teaches us to "ask," "seek," and "knock" (Matthew 7:7). So, why just accept the status quo?

Yet, the problem with both views is that they fly against the reality, as most persons who converse, when either or both happen to be in the Single Adult grouping, know full well that sooner or later, someone will ask, "<u>So, how's your love life</u>?"

If you definitely are not looking, or, at the very least, slowing down to be looked at, this chapter may be a blessing to you, in that it will let you know, when the time is right. Like all things, I call upon you to give your serious consideration to this material. "Weigh" it in your heart, mind and spirit. Some suggested steps to take in choosing a marital partner:

1. <u>To look for a mate is not un-spiritual</u>.
   Consider Proverbs 18:22. "He who finds a wife finds a good thing...."
   Tell me, friend, how one "finds" without "searching."
   If the inspired, authoritative Word of God tells a man (or woman) to look for this "good thing," shouldn't we accept it as from the Lord?
   Most important key: that one looks in the right place!
   More and more, spiritual people must utilize spiritual resources and methods. Dating services thrive because there are millions of eligible Singles, hoping for a "<u>love connection</u>." There is nothing inherently wrong with such methods, but, for the Christian, there are other ways to "search."

2. <u>To desire your choice of a mate is not secular</u>.
   Read Psalm 84:11. "No good thing does He withhold from those who walk uprightly."
   We must wage a war against those who give the impression that one is wrong for stating a preference for the type of wife or husband desired in this life search. If you accept the premise that, "He's a good provider" or "She's good with children" or "My family likes him/her," what you may do is set yourself up for a bad experience later.
   The point is, just because you "settle" for something in a mate does not take away your ideal person. What happens, unwittingly, is that we tend to push such a person to be what he/she cannot be. Various physical attributes cannot be altered. Also, there are inherent traits which another is not able to change. But, if your ideal is not found, then you are likely to hear, later on, "I am sorry I can't be what you want from me." There is hope for

all, nevertheless.

Since "one man's trash is another man's treasure," and since we are "attracted" to different looks, styles, attitudes, ways, sizes, and shapes, there is no objective standard as to a "perfect" choice. Remember: "Beauty is only skin deep; but ugly is to the bone!"

Choices vary, thus each person should pursue the woman or man of their dreams. Also, note that the person you marry will change physically, emotionally, mentally, spiritually, and socially. You can be certain of that fact. Knowing the inevitability of "change," you should seek to find someone with whom you, despite the changes, can live happily together forever.

3. Any anxiety which such a concern produces should be a matter of prayer.

Refer to Matthew 6:25-34.

Refer to Philippians 4:6-8.

Refer to I Peter 5:7.

These passages teach a central truth: the kingdom of God should be of utmost concern for the child of God. Be sure that nothing, including a need for a godly mate, interferes with this. If you are ever given an ultimatum, "Me or the church," I trust that you will show that person the door very quickly. Any mate, and especially any mate that God sanctions, will cause you to grow closer to the Lord, rather than further away.

Prayer for a mate means that you ask God to equip you for the person He has for you. Any delay between request and granting may be the time God uses in the preparatory period. Ask, as well, a friend, in confidence, to stand in agreement with you over this matter. When God answers, the two of you may rejoice and praise Him for the victory.

4. Christian Single Adults have a God-ordained means of finding a mate.

Whatever the world at large uses as a means of choosing a friend, a mate, a lover, a companion, a wife, a husband, will not suffice if you take seriously your relationship with Christ. He has a higher, more noble standard for such a serious commitment.

Over and again, we should be brought back to the truth that what we face in this life really matters to the Lord. That the period of singlehood is fraught with bouts of severe loneliness is a source of concern to Him. Even as He may give you a mate, more critically is that you find in God the relationship you need. No partner, no wife, no husband can take the space reserved for God.

5. <u>Maturity, not peer pressure, age or desire, should prompt the search</u>.

   Marriage is too important to make it just another decision to make, in the off-hand way we do other things.

   When I refer to maturity, I mean the ability to accept responsibility, the knowledge of the nature of commitment, the capacity to set the needs, wishes and desires of another beyond one's own, and more.

   How many couples have had to marry the old time "shot-gun weddings," before either party was ready, with the result being that one or both has felt locked in because all of one's youth has been taken by "adult" responsibilities?

   Some time ago, I counseled with a couple seeking marriage. The man continually expressed his fear of taking the step. But, the couple had purchased a home together, and had even begun to decorate and furnish it. The woman kept assuring her fiancé of the jitters and cold feet all get about such things. Hearing this discussion, I became quite concerned that perhaps they should wait awhile. I expressed this and we agreed they would talk more between themselves. They called and convinced me that all was well. For some reason I couldn't shake the thought that something was not quite right. A few months after the wedding, I learned that they had separated.

The moral is: wait, pray, wait, ask, seek the will of God, pray, wait, until major doubts are settled. Don't push yourself or another into so momentous a decision.

6. <u>One should look for the following attributes in a Christian mate</u>:

   A. Evidence of having had <u>a new birth experience with Jesus Christ</u>, wherein this experience touches all areas of life, up to this present moment.

   Turn to <u>2 Corinthians 6:14-16</u>. Do you accept it for life?

   <u>Questions</u>: Does he/she attend worship regularly? Does he/she pray to God as the Bible declares Him? Does he/she practice Tithing? Does he/she accept the Bible as the truth as well as guide for life? Is he/she honest?

   In the real world we live in, persons of different faiths meet. The question becomes, should one marry outside the faith? The short answer is No! The reason for such a strong statement is that the marriage may not withstand being pulled in two distinct directions. A Christian should pause before getting involved with a Muslim, a Buddhist, a Jehovah's Witness, a Religious Scientist, a New Age student, or some other religion. Also, should children later come to the marital relationship, what teaching would they receive? These are vital issues which demand your careful consideration before you say, "I will" to the proposal.

   B. A <u>healthy self-image</u> (refer to chapter) and outlook on life.

   Consider <u>Proverbs 23:7</u>.

   In the process of oneness, if a partner always feels depression, failure, fatalism, despair, anger, and bizarre thoughts, it is bound to be shared with the

mate. Free-floating emotions such as these may produce a difficult person with which to live.

C. A balanced <u>sense of humor</u> and ability to <u>laugh</u>.
Look at <u>Proverbs 17:22</u>.
Norman Cousins, so the story goes, checked out of
the hospital with a serious, life-threatening illness,
and into a nice hotel nearby. He then began to fill
up on funny stories and jokes. A short time later, he
had "laughed" himself back to health.
In times like these, no one wants a dull, lifeless, kill-
joy as a mate. Life is too short. Find someone with
a ready smile. Christianity is not how much one
can frown, because the Bible talks a lot about <u>JOY</u>!
<u>Relax, and enjoy the walk with God</u>!

D. <u>Compassion for all people</u>, especially the needy.
Read <u>Colossians 3:12-17</u>. Does it make sense?
The wedding vow holds that marriage is for
"richer or poorer, in sickness or in health, until
death us do part," which calls for a loving, generous individual.
<u>Questions</u>: Could you take care of this person were
he/she to fall ill, as happened to a couple I married
in their late 30s. She bathed him, sat with him, fed
him and more. Do you think he/she would do that
for you?

E. A dynamic life of <u>faith</u> in the power, perspective of
God.
Turn to <u>Hebrews 11:1, 6</u>. Can you live without faith?
The significance of a person having faith has to do
with those times when a couple will have to trust
God, perhaps at a crisis moment, or when the finances are low, or when you both want to give up
on the marriage, as there are not ready answers to
life's perplexities.

F. The ability to <u>call on God (pray)</u> for direction, guid-
    ance.
    Look at <u>Matthew 6:6-13</u>. Will you accept God's
    model?
    If a person commits to prayer, many of the challenges
    become manageable because God gives greater un-
    derstanding, along with the ability to wait for His
    answers.

G. An acceptance of <u>biblically-defined roles</u> in the
    home.
    Evaluate <u>Ephesians 5:21 - 6:4</u>. What are its prin-
    ciples?
    Can you really accept what God says you are to be
    as a Christian husband/wife? Do you believe your
    prospective mate will honor the role assigned?
    In the "give" and "take" of a marital relationship,
    there must be a knowledge of the place of each per-
    son in relation to the other, within love and affirma-
    tion.
    "<u>Obey</u>" is the greatest challenge for a wife because
    it calls for an acceptance of her husband as the leader
    of the home.
    "<u>Love</u>" is the greatest challenge for a husband be-
    cause, under normal conditions, he would only be
    concerned with his own needs. Also, to "love as
    Christ loved the church" poses a high standard for
    a Christian husband.
    <u>Nowhere in Scripture are we given a definitive how-
    to on finding a Christian mate. What we do have
    are examples of good and poor choices, and the
    implications of each.</u>

A. Read Genesis 24 - "arranged marriage" for Isaac
B. Read Genesis 29 - "physical attraction" by Jacob
C. Read Exodus 2:21 - "arranged marriage" for Moses

D. Read Judges 14 - "physical attraction" for Samson
E. Read 2 Samuel 2 - "lust" by David
F. Read 1 Kings 3:1 - "political alliance" for Solomon
G. Read Song of Solomon - "love and romance" as ideal for couple
H. Read Hosea 1 - "model of God's love for His own" for Hosea
I. Read John 4 - "rash, quick choices" by unnamed woman at well
J. Read Acts 18:2 - "shared spiritual interests" for Ananias/Saphira

While we have, from the above passages, no sure "road map" for our selections, we do have the following principles: <u>choices</u> lead to <u>content</u> which leads to <u>consequences</u> which shape <u>character</u>. It all begins with our "free will" choice, which God gives, but for which we shall be responsible.

8. <u>Following represents my personal reasoned judgment, after several years in the pastorate, substantial marital counseling sessions with many, observations of numerous couple (before and after marriage) and the wisdom from the Holy Spirit as to finding a Christian mate</u>.

I wholeheartedly affirm all the points made above, especially #6 relative to the peculiarities of a Christian mate.

In addition, one must seek a person who "rings your bell" in that you feel that "Cupid" or somebody shot you. Yes, it ought to be an emotional matter, one which you may or may not be able to fully explain. Try as you might to explain, you just "love" the other person, with an honest appraisal of what you're getting. Some will take offense with this position because it seems as if I have some naive notion of "and they lived happily ever after" simply because there was a "feeling" in the stomach.

I AM NOT ADVOCATING THAT KIND OF LOVE!

However, since we know that love ebbs and flows, comes and goes, shouldn't one at least <u>start out</u> with feelings of bliss? Plus, I believe this with all my heart, if you start searching for certain physical, mental, intellectual and other feature, and then "settle" for less, what happens (now you're married) when you meet someone who has it "all"?

<u>Food for Thought</u>: Could the basis for some extra-marital affairs be that we married one type of person while really harboring a desire for a different type of person, who now works with us, attends our church, lives down the block or what-have-you?

My pious friends will say, in reply, "But when you're saved you resist the temptation and stay with your wife." My reply: "Yeah, but haven't you read about some escapades lately even among Christians?" Too many people take their vows for granted. We should seek to avoid the trek down the road to infidelity by getting all we desire in a husband/wife, thus preventing the need to seek "whatever" in the arms of another.

9. <u>There must be a willingness to wait for God's timing</u>. Read Isaiah 40:28-31. Are these words for Single Adults? There is agreement between the Word of God and sociologists who speak of "deferred gratification," by which they mean the ability to postpone certain pleasures to a time when they can be enjoyed, rather than moving before time.

<u>A practical thought which comes to mind often</u>: many young couples plan pre-marital counseling sessions <u>after</u> setting a date, buying a wedding ring, putting a down payment on the dress, engaging a local caterer, sending out announcements, booking a hotel for guests, and a hundred other important acts. Might some continue with the wedding plans (even as counseling brings out the inadvisability of marriage for this couple) simply because of the expense already incurred, as well as

potential embarrassment?

What if both thought it out, prayed it out, talked it out, and then, convinced of the Lord's hand in it, set about to move towards marriage.

10. <u>Get as much information as you can, from as many sources as possible, relative to his/her habits, pet peeves, fetishes, idiosyncrasies, moods, dislikes, ways, tempers, fears, phobias and more</u>.

How does your Romeo/Juliet handle stress, pressure, anger, setbacks, defeats, bad news, unrealized expectations, criticism, uncertainty, and more?

Let us remember that marriage is a life-long commitment! Therefore, you should strive to really "know" the other person. Such knowledge can come through observation, questions, discussions, and the unbiased views of close friends.

Some have said, and I really believe it, "<u>You don't really know a person until you live with them as husband and wife</u>."

Let's face it, that's scary! How many have married a Dr. Jekyll/Mr. Hyde to their regret. Only by prayer and observation and questions can we have a sense of who we're getting involved with.

Also, during courtship and engagement, most couples are on their best behavior, with their brightest smiles, freshest breath, total manners, and winningest attitudes, those who know tell us and more.

Those who know tell us it doesn't (though one could at least try) last beyond when they say "I do." (The beerbelly is held in until after the wedding, then it and the ripped T-shirt become the regular attire.)

11. <u>Solicit the advice of friends, family, pastor, spiritual mentors and others as to their beliefs as to the advisability of your marriage to a particular person</u>.

Why must we persist with the macho, I-can-handle-this, lone ranger posture? Why not admit, to self and others, that this is a big step, wherein we need guidance, prayer and help from outside ourselves?

I fear that some will think me overly cautious; yet, it simply stems from the serious nature of marriage and the lazy manner in which we approach such a quality decision and quantity commitment.

Point: <u>When 1 out of 2 marriages ends in divorce, even a fool can see that people are making disastrous choices</u>! Read Proverbs 12:15; 13:10; 20:5. What does this say to you? There is an all-important advisement: <u>ultimately the decision will be a singular one</u>. No one can really "decide" for you.

12. <u>Be realistic in the search for a mate by accepting the imperfections of others and self</u>.

The total biblical witness confirms the fact that all persons are products of the falseness of humanity, from Adam, with the result that we all have evidence of the fall. Even those who have been saved are, at best, sinners saved by grace, yet the emphasis should be on "sinners," thus, there is no such thing as the perfectibility of persons.

<u>My biggest surprise has been that I'm not perfect (smile)</u>. If that recognition has not come to you, let me be the first to tell you, "Brother, you are not perfect!" "Sister, you are not perfect!"

13. <u>Pray that you find, in this search, a godly mate</u>.

Read Proverbs 31:10-31. Does she sound like anyone you know?

Make this person the standard. Recognize that this person will be a "diamond in the rough." To find her/him is to discover a true treasure.

14. <u>Learn how to "court" once you find a good prospect for marriage</u>.

Refer to Song of Solomon 1-3. Find the ways to practice courting. We need to be reminded that every sane person enjoys flowers, cards, candy, trinkets, calls and more, as reflections of growing affection.

Be thoughtful, creative, spontaneous and honest. Don't do any more than you can continue after the courtship is over. No one wants to feel as if he/she is being "bought." Take the courtship as a "discovery" phase. The word "dating" is in the family of "data," (gathering bits of information). Don't be hasty. Give it time to develop. Ask questions and await the answers. Open your new friend up to old friends. How do they get along? Is it comfortable? At some point, this individual should be introduced to your parents, not necessarily for "inspection," but only for friendship. How is it so far? If good, continue on that <u>slow</u> path.

Slowly broach the subject of an exclusive commitment. If all still seems within the will of God, continue in prayer and discussion of what marriage would be like. (Refer back to the chapter on "Foundations for Marriage").

15. <u>Knowing what you do, committing your way to God, set the date</u>!

Is it too late to turn back? What if I'm making a mistake? What have I got myself into? Can I really go through with this?

<u>Prudence dictates that you, at least, have an engagement period of from 3-6 months, or longer</u>. For some persons it should be a year or two. You must wait until you feel comfortable. A friend shared an experience which he swears is true. He asked a young lady for a date several times, to no avail, as she repeatedly turned him down. Finally, he asked once again. The pattern was the same until he said, "You don't have to go out with me because one day we'll be married; then we will have many opportunities to go out."

Suffice it to say, they have been happily married now for many years. He was patient in getting a date, but when he finally got it, the date was for a lifetime!

REBOUNDING AND REBUILDING

The great unmentionable in the Singles Ministry of many churches is the D-word, "divorce." It conjures up failure, loss, mistaken commitment, shame, and the death of a relationship. How many in our pews, week after week, carry the burden of a painful divorce, but who are afraid to express their hurt? It is now time for the Christian community to provide the divorced among the family a way to re-enter the mainstream of the life of God's Church.

Initially, it would be a great benefit if more of the leadership of the Church would make the divorced feel welcomed to the family of God by providing a warm, loving and affirming atmosphere. Where there is a spirit of forgiveness, all persons may come to the Lord Jesus Christ, with a desire to experience His acceptance.

During His earthly ministry, Christ faced people of all walks of life, but He spent an unusual amount of time among the hurting, so much so that He was ridiculed for His love of "sinners." The religious establishment was the target of His stinging rebuke because they did not evidence the requisite concern for the hurting. Where they shunned those who had experienced one of life's hurts, the Master called the "weary and heavy-laden" to Himself.

This, then, must form the basis for the ministry to the divorced. They should not be viewed as the "untouchables," nor the social "pariahs," who, because of an emotional breakup, have no place in the family of God. Any spirit which shuns the divorced in our churches is evil, repugnant, and sinful.

Repeatedly, whenever Christ came in contact with one whose dreams had been crushed by the realities of relational upheaval, He was at once caring, for He knew the human propensity toward hurt, and was prepared to lift such a person out of the prison of despair. He always sought to reconstruct the emotional landscape of one who needed an affirming word.

In the Gospel of John, chapter 8, we discover a riveting episode in which Jesus furnishes us abundant resources for the underlying principle by which He went about reestablishing the person when one fell into sin. How He treated the woman here says a great deal about His attitude toward the divorced and the hurt among our churches.

According to words of the Scribes and Pharisees, at the time, the known punishment for the sin named, the witnesses, and the clear evidence, the Master knew the woman to be an adulteress. He could, therefore, act in one of three ways: 1) <u>Condemn Her</u> (as the religious establishment had done; 2) <u>Condone Her</u> (which would allow the woman to get out of punishment; or 3) <u>Confront Her.</u> (Express that her act was sin, but she could still receive love from the Lord.

For too long the Christian church has followed the Pharisaic model, by condemning good people for relational breakdowns (divorces), rather than the model of the Head of the Church, the Lord Jesus Christ, who yet again separates sinner from sin. Rightly, He tells the woman, "Neither do I condemn you; go your way. From now on sin no more."

Notice that there is a positive air about the Master's encounter with the woman to the extent that she leaves Him knowing that God yet cares, even when we fall.

When challenged by the religionists, Jesus Christ would not be baited into a quick analysis of the woman. In an act which biblical scholars cannot fully fathom, nor adequately interpret, He simply wrote on the ground. Since there are any number of suggestions as to what He wrote, allow me to suggest another, equally valid, since we will never know for sure.

Perhaps, the Lord wrote that day, which we may apply

to the divorced, "Please be patient with her; God is not finished with her yet!"

Furthermore, in the John 4 encounter with the woman at the well of Sychar, again Jesus seeks to confront the sinner, in love, as well as extending God's affirmation, so as to maintain the person as a part of humanity, for whom Christ would, ultimately, be willing to give His life. Christ challenged the shallow commitment of the woman, evident by the ease with which she procured five husbands. She needed a lesson in true love and fidelity, rather than condemnation.

The best indicator as to whether one truly understands the way of the Master can be seen by the immediate aftermath of coming in contact with Him. The adulterer went her way forgiven, with a heavy burden lifted. The woman at the well went away telling all of the One who seeks to redeem humanity. As a result, "many believed."

Only the affirmed search out those who need the healing touch of a word from Jesus Christ. As His body, can we treat those who are hurting in any other way?

Let us take such principles, with the express intention of applying them to a "rebuilding ministry" in the body of Christ (the church).

<u>What happens, emotionally, to one who experiences a divorce</u>?

While every relationship is unique, there are some generalities which pastors/ministers, marriage counselors, psychologists, therapists, and those for whom it is a reality, would conclude occurs in a divorce.

First, there is the sense of tremendous loss, as one accepts that a marriage is irreparably and irretrievably severed, often well before the legal divorce takes place. Most mature persons have tried to talk to their mates, obtain counseling, read good books, and question others, yet, it seems as if there is no other way. So, some precipitating event or date rolls around, and the couple moves toward the divorce.

The loss may take the form of a realization that the special friend is gone. Even when a marriage is bad, according to many, there still remains a hope that, somehow, someway, it will get better. So, for months, for years, the couple gives time and effort, but, after all that, the inevitable appears: we cannot be together. The loss, then, can be a very strong emotion with which to cope.

Second, there may be the emotion of guilt, for now one must face life in the shadow of a failed relationship. A child or children, friends, family, in-laws, and others who knew of the couple must now assess the individual. One faces the paralyzing issue of explaining to persons with whom we have shared much in the past, the news of the breakup. It calls upon one to accept responsibility for the rupture.

Directly related, one feels the eyes of the world turned toward the breakup. It seems like there is universal disapproval of one's act. Perhaps this feeling stems from the fact that a marriage is a public commitment, made usually in a church or chapel setting. So, when a divorce occurs, one is guilty because he/she has "let everybody down."

Third, there may be deep frustration because one gave one's all, yet the marriage failed. Here, one may feel cheated, as the other may not have tried with the same intensity. Or, one may feel that the other didn't fully comprehend the nature of the commitment, in the eyes of God, or to another.

The complexity of conversation following a divorce makes it difficult to do a "post-mortem" examination (medical terminology for autopsy the cause of death) on the reasons for the breach in the relationship, thus, the frustration continues without adequate resolution.

Fourth, directly related, there may be palpable anger. A thousand questions leap to the surface: "Why was I so unlucky in love?" "How could this happen to me?" "Why this and why now?" "How will this divorce affect the children?" "How dare you steal my sense of joy?" "Where do I go from here?" "Who will want me now?" "Does God forgive divorce?" "How do I choose new friends?" "How do I date after all these years?" "What does my future hold?"

When one cannot communicate this anger to the source to which it should be directed, both toward self and the mate, then the result will be a deepening of the anger. In order to move forward, of course, one must face the anger. For a believer, the best way to cope with anger is to express it, by one's prayer life, with the assurance that God will alleviate it.

Fifth, there may be a sense of rejection, especially when there is a divorce request which seems to come without warning. An example may be the recent revelation of an extra-marital affair, or a child sired outside the bonds of marriage. These events may plunge an individual into despair and disillusionment, as the marriage partner seems to totally reject the personhood of the mate.

Again, we must remember that marital status begins to intertwine with our concept of self-esteem and self-worth. Not surprisingly, then, the absence of the mate can take one into new, unexplored territory. It becomes a frightening trek into the unknown. All of this befalls one in isolation.

Sixth, there may be disorientation. Whatever length of time one was involved in a marital relationship, certain patterns developed. A certain rhythm came into play. Now, with the end of the marriage, there are new places to go, new friends to meet, new habits to adopt, new customs to embrace, and all of that may present a significant source of disorientation.

Seventh, there is the trauma, which we take from medical research. Here, the individual may suffer an injury, a wound, which may bring about a neurosis, with a lasting psychic effect. To some degree, then, one's emotional hurt has an accompanying physical manifestation. In layman's words, "It hurts to be divorced."

For those who have "been there," there are nights of pain, where the ache of the breakup feels quite intense. Tears come, emotions race in a hundred directions, and clear thinking becomes difficult. All of this because a divorce is one of life's most unsettling "transitions."

Finally, there may be an emotion akin to what occurs when a relative or close friend dies. This may be termed grief, and all that accompanies physical death may ensue for the divorced. One may call for the other, expecting to hear that familiar voice, to no avail. One may get in bed, expecting the mate to follow, as in other times, but the wife/ husband never shows. One may set the table for a meal, with a place for the husband, as in other days, but dinner must be eaten alone. The mail may still be addressed to the one who has moved on. (The change of address form was not readily processed.). Any reminder of the former spouse sets off a range of emotions.

Perhaps it will be a song, a picture, a special place and time, but the feelings flourish anew, for you were making a life with another, but, now, it's gone. Memories are funny things in that they reappear without warning. Psychologists speak of "repressed memories," which are those we attempt to bury, yet they return at the worst times, and cry out for resolution.

Clearly, the above will not exhaust all that one feels in the time after a divorce. The items are merely an attempt to acquaint us with the "roller coaster" of emotions one may experience. In some cases, we hear of "amicable" divorces. They may occur, but it is highly unlikely or rare.

Louis Nizer, famous attorney, summarizes the issue of divorce thusly:

"Litigation between husbands and wives exceed bitterness and hatred those of any other relationships. I leave it to psychiatrists the explanation of the volatile transformation from love to hate. There is a mysterious element, which unbalances the mind, changes the personality, and distorts the character... Two people joined together in intimacy are often like Siamese twins, the separation of one causing the death of the other..."

From that secular analysis, we can discern that a great

deal is at work in the cognitive circuitry (the mind) as one goes through the emotionally wrenching experience of a divorce. What he, and others, tell us about divorce should cause the Christian Church to look anew at those in our pews who must face life with emotional scar tissue called a divorce.

In the title of this chapter, a metaphor is employed, rebounding, which takes us to the arena of athletics, namely, basketball, which uses the term for a missed shot, which caroms off the rim, and which the shooter or another catches. Think about the idea of rebound in the context of divorce, and one begins to understand that life is not over for the divorced. The rebound process must be faced, and, when one is so engaged, the real healing can begin.

How can one "rebound" from a divorce?

Initially, like all situations fraught with the potential for growth, in a divorce, one must accept that the marriage is over, if this is the mutually agreed upon course of action on the part of both parties. Husband/wife is gone! The two will never be one! There is no use fighting the truth: the love, the joy, the hope, the plans, the dreams - all are gone! This is how, for the two, the story ends! (Sadly, there are those who cannot accept that the marriage is over. Such persons cling to the hope of reconciliation, up to the point that the former spouse remarries. In such thinking, the result is delayed healing.)

The cold stark reality of the above paragraph is meant to present the divorced persons with the new life choices available. One can either remain mired in the consideration of what was, or one can move into the bright sunshine of what can be. In the former there will be constant regret, while in the latter there can be new fulfillment. The choice remains with us.

When the tears flow, recognize that they are the release of emotions. It is good that we have the capacity to express our grief, for it serves as a means of lowering the pain threshold. Even the Lord Jesus cried on one occasion. So, when we cry, we vent our deep hurt. So, cry until the tears stop flowing. But, after the tears, begin the long process of recovery, with the understanding that we have the freedom to take our time in a healing "process." The idea of process always carries with it the element of time.

Healing, then, from a divorce is not so much a destination, but the enjoyment of the journey toward wholeness. We must rid our thinking that we were "there" before, during or after marriage. Life, in itself, is a long process of "becoming." In that sense, we will never "get there," but thank God for the journey!

As alluded to above, divorce can be likened to a death, so the mourning period follows after the declaration, made in heady moments, "I am just glad this marriage is over!" No serious, sane individual can quickly "bounce back" from a marriage, in the way that many attempt to convey with their brave words and defiant posturing.

We must start at the point of a devastating experience. Once completed, the next step may be sorting out what one should expect. (All the emotions delineated above, interacting one with the other, in a crazy fashion.) Give oneself time to "get it together."

Since we are speaking of an emotional, psychological, mental and spiritual recovery, we will need all the resources available to us, both human and divine. In other words, this is the time when many discover that God is "a very present help in trouble" (Psalm 46). Thus, by all means, He should be the Source of healing and all comfort. Like a thread in a garment, may the truth rest on you, that, "God cares for you!" In dark moments, He responds best.

At the same time, too many persons going through a divorce run away from the Body of Christ, the Church, because of the agony, pain, guilt and hurt they feel. Such a response prevents healing, for the Christian family is the one place where all should feel warmth, love and understanding. God's people should be the most affirming. One should not assume that the local congregation will not open her arms to the divorced. After all, the Church is defined, both in Scripture and praxis, as the "caring community," and, if she abrogates such a role, she seriously calls into question her relevance to hurting persons.

Whatever else the Church may be, it is still the first place one ought go for hope and a practical "word from the Lord," which may be revealed through the preaching, the music ministry, the Singles group, the aged saint, the praying brother, or the wise mother. I challenge you, divorced friend, to find that person who will follow the biblical admonition, "Bear one another's burdens, and thus fulfill the law of Christ" (Galatians 6:2).

This is not the time for the seemingly helpful, yet hurtful, time of "spiritual exile," as one reasons, "I'll just stay home for awhile and get myself together." For too long, Satan has used that trick to trap so many sincere followers of God. What the devil does is to get the hurting saint (isolated) in a position where you fall prey to self-pity, doubt God's love, harbor anger toward successful couples, and become resentful for your lot in life. Alone, away from the resources given to the Body of Christ, you wallow in the muck of your breakup.

Extensive counseling may be recommended, as well, to allow one to "vent" in an atmosphere which is non-judgmental. There are trained psychologists who may have the tools to help you begin again, after a painful period in your life. We cannot be afraid nor hesitant to seek the services of these professionals, for they may be a vital link in the chain of one's future development. It is best, however, if one can come under Christian counseling, or at least one who utilizes a Christian-based approach.

In the main, however, the thesis driving this chapter is that one need not face this catastrophe alone. For too long, we have been ill-advised to adopt the stiff-upper-lip, I-can-handle-this-alone approach. Such reasoning fails to include the numerous other loving persons (family, friends, fellow church members, others in Singles Ministry and unknown others) who may be there with a sympathetic ear or shoulder for our hurts.

Rebuilding occurs, nevertheless, in the context of a healthy understanding of what one has passed through, along with a sense of what one seeks in the new, evolving process. One must avoid, in this regard, further abusive behavior.

Overeating, alcoholic beverages, one-night stands, clubs/partying, a quick new relationship, drugs, and more are definitely not to be considered as helpful to moving towards emotional health for the recently divorced. While the foregoing may provide a temporary distraction from the pain, nothing in that listing provides a permanent solution to the deeper malady.

To take one example, the single man at the bar, on the make for a single woman, willing to buy an endless supply of drinks is, in reality, deeply pained, trying to gain some validation of self. He may take someone home for that night, but the pain yet lingers!

Further, to engage in such behavior only leads to other problems. So, in attempting to cope with the loneliness and despair, one now has other issues with which to cope. One may, therefore, find life spiraling out of control. Tragic, indeed, would be the result!

A better way to "rebuild" is to take the time after divorce as an evaluative one, to assess, to develop a better sense of self-worth. Spend more time with those you trust, as such friends and family will furnish invaluable positive feedback. (It is not helpful, however, to hear only from those who support you in blaming your mate for the breakup. Such "sounding boards" should be objective and impartial, to the degree any friend or family can be. Otherwise, you are left in a state of anger and denial.)

Stuart Fishoff, a psychology professor, points out that, "men and women bleed in different ways." Of course, he speaks of the manner in which their hurt is manifested. Since more women than men define their self-image by virtue of the relationship, it tends to be the case that women will exhibit more hurt in the aftermath of a marital rupture.

In summary, then, the rebuilding phase can be viewed in a positive light, for it allows one to acquire problem-solving skills for the defense of subsequent relationships. When you discover the seeds of failure, you then decide where you can and cannot "plant" them in new soil.

Overall, one is advised to use the post-breakup period to be nice to yourself. Treat yourself in the manner you would like to be treated by someone else. Practically speaking, you have the right to take a long walk, ride a bike, read a great novel, take frequent bubble baths, take a trip, go to the movies by yourself, or even a candlelight dinner in an exclusive restaurant.

Another means of "release" may be to compose a journal of your thoughts. Write down your feelings and look over the pages for new discoveries about yourself, with whom you are being reacquainted after existing in a couple. After a few days or weeks, you may surprise yourself by how much you have grown in your capacity to face new challenges. Turn whatever destructive thoughts you have into constructive ones. In so doing, you may discover important steps along the journey.

A vital question in the minds of many divorced persons, including Christian Singles, is a simple one: "<u>Does God allow for remarriage for the divorced</u>?"

To answer the question directly, we need to note that, first, God instituted marriage to be an exclusive, monogamous, permanent relationship between one husband and one wife. So, in a narrow sense, He does not allow for divorce, let alone remarriage.

Having said that, we must factor into our consideration of remarriage the fallen condition, the sinful nature, the propensity toward our own will, that so characterizes all of humanity, necessitating the redemptive work of Jesus Christ on the Cross. As sinful creatures, we find ourselves, even believers, in situations where we have strayed from God's ideal. Thus, those who are now divorced.

Once divorced, we must consider the person as a saint of God whose sin hinders the fellowship, but not the relationship, with the Father. 1 John 1:9 gives the only remedial measure such a person can take, if the Lord is to be pleased. When we "confess" our sins, He restores the joy and fellowship with His own.

So, it is critical that any divorced person take the failure of the marriage to God, in honesty and seriousness, with a request that He will forgive and cleanse. Such a person should be forthright in his/her sin (which characterizes the scriptural view of divorce) well before one gives any consideration to what happens next.

In Jesus Christ, then, we have restoration, with a renewed sense of God's love for us, for when He forgives, He "puts back" in places of service. Therefore, all persons, even the divorced who have confessed their inability to live up to the Master's ideal, may be restored in love and affirmation.

The answer to the question raised above about remarriage must consider the truths derived from a reading of several passages, including Deuteronomy 24:1-4; Jeremiah 3:8; Malachi 2:16; Matthew 5:31,32; Matthew 19:9; Romans 7:2,3; I Corinthians 7:2,3; and other texts.

From these passages, we learn that since God did not ordain divorce, He equally does not ordain remarriage. The two concepts are intertwined. Yet, even when the ideal is missed, there is still the person in question.

<u>Remarriage, I believe, from the total witness of Scripture, should be viewed as a viable option for those believers who have come to an understanding of God's ideal, even as they may have failed in a previous marital commitment</u>. What we should strive for is to learn from the mistakes of the initial coupling, so as to know how to prevent future problems.

David Hocking, in the book, <u>Marrying Again</u>, makes

many important contributions to this discussion; namely, that thoughts of remarriage should be grounded in a proper understanding of the marital commitment. (One contemplating remarriage should read this book, among others, for greater insight.)

The word "adultery" frightens many, as the Word makes it plain that the person who divorces and remarries engages in this. We should not minimize what Christ said, nor should we lock a person into such an emotional "straightjacket." Perhaps we should focus on the attitude rather than the state of the adultery. All unrighteousness is sin, so adultery should be viewed in that sense. All sin must be confessed before the Father.

The Lord loves all persons, so we would do well to call all to maintain a strong view of the marriage ideal, while keeping in mind that those who fail yet need to know there is a possibility for recovery, and remarriage.

(Clearly, we cannot exhaust the subject here, for there is much left to be said. The complexity of the topic, and the limitations of space and time, only allow us to skim the surface. I highly recommend further reading in this most important area.)

Suffice to say, <u>there is hope for the divorced</u>. They can lead valuable, productive lives, even in the life of the Christian Church. The Singles Ministry should be a place for affirmation, forgiveness, understanding and rebuilding.

Our challenge is to make the Body of Christ the place where all can come, bringing their emotional baggage, which may constitute a heavy burden. When such persons come, divorced, abused, battered by life, may they find that we have the "balm" for their suffering.

In the Lord Jesus Christ, all can come to the haven of hope; the refuge for the restless; and the source for solace. In the Church, we epitomize the concern of our Christ. We personify the character of the Savior. Our very reason for existence (raison d'être) is inextricably woven into being that caring presence for all humanity.

CAREER DEVELOPMENT

For the Christian Single, there is an important link between one's place in the economic order, derived primarily from one's job or career, and we should carefully consider what steps we take in relating to that all important function.

No one can successfully dispute the assertion that there is a direct correlation between work and life. In order to live, and have the things needed for survival in this culture, one must have a means of gainful employment. Whenever we meet another, we ask or prepare to be asked about the line of work we're in.

(An oft-repeated story has a single woman saying she desires a BMW. Of course, the response was, "That's a great car!" To which she replies, "Not that kind of BMW. I want a Black Man Working!")

Even the Bible teaches the blessing of work, as 2 Thessalonians 3:10, written almost 2,000 years ago, declares: "For even when we were with you, we used to give you this order: "If anyone will not work, neither let him eat." Or, no work, no eat. So, work is sanctioned from Adam to the present.

Beyond this, however, I want to posit the view that employment should be more than simply a job; there is the need for a relation in the workplace which engages the mind and the body.

How do you develop a career of fulfillment? How do you get out of a dead-end job? How do you find true satisfaction in your work? How do you deepen the relationships with your co-workers? How do you get that raise from your boss?

In a given 24-hour period, one sleeps a third of the time; eats, drinks, plays, relaxes, thinks, plans and more a third of the time; and then works a third of the time.

We, therefore, give time to <u>Recuperation</u> (sleep); <u>Recreation</u> (eat/play); and <u>Remuneration</u> (work/reward).

In light of such a large portion of time being given to employment, it stands to reason that one would derive more than a paycheck and the fringe benefits thereof.

At the outset, it should be noted that there is a difference between who one is (self-worth) and what one may happen to do (role-playing), which means that we are more than the job classification, whether one is president, senior v.p., manager, secretary, clerk, doctor, attorney, mail supervisor, custodian, scientist, chief cook, or bottle washer.

Note, moreover, that every believer in Jesus Christ takes "life" from his/her relationship with the Source. God infuses our personhood with infinite worth and value. Thus, even if the job is taken away, one yet retains value.

1. If you are doing the job that serves a larger interest than simply making more money from some faceless conglomerate, then, you can expect to have a degree of joy in doing it.

2. When you put "self" into the job, which means the engagement of all your talents and abilities in order to carry out the task, the hope will be that you will gain a commensurate benefit.

3. Have you been specifically trained for the job you do, based on your time spent in high school, college, graduate school? If so, the likelihood is that you are content with your present position.

4. In all areas of human endeavor, the inescapable reality which stands before us is that of racism. It is personal, endemic, pervasive, systemic and institutional. It keeps the best minds down. It takes away the hope of advancement beyond a certain point ("glass ceiling.") It dehumanizes those who dream of better standing in the "pecking order."

5. There are numerous ways to climb the ladder of success, most of which entail social relationships outside the workplace. "Who you know" works more so than "what you know." Use this knowledge to develop healthy, platonic (non-sexual) relationships.

6. In many corporations, the menace of drug abuse will mean that after the mandatory testing many will lose jobs because of practices done outside the job.

7. Productivity quotients measure what is expected without focusing on the individual, with the result that those who cannot produce find themselves victims of lay-offs and cutbacks.

8. The single best determiner for career development is still education and training in specific areas. Make it a point to be a continual learner. Be aggressive in accepting new challenges and responsibilities. Take Saturday and night school classes to advance skills and technical competency. Prepare for the "information superhighway" of the 90s and beyond. The 21st Century is upon us.

9. Affirmative-action laws are being questioned as never before, with the United States Supreme Court holding that such programs constitute what they call "reverse discrimination." The white Anglo male now claims victimization. Any African American advances are classified as "preferential treatment" or "quotas."

10. Those who believe that unions will fight for their rights should consider the anti-union climate in which many companies operate. Even the venerable American business of baseball considered "replacement players" during the baseball strike of the mid 90s. Clearly, "strike-busting" is in.

11. The wise worker will be on the lookout for new opportunities for advancement, and will actively ask for greater responsibilities so as to build one's capabilities. Singles have the freedom to relocate to new cities as the career takes off.

12. Often the means of getting a promotion is to show a work record of punctuality, hard work, honesty, few absences and team spirit. Resist the temptation to do less than one's best. Make work a reflection of your sense of integrity. Although it seems quaint, the best policy is, "An honest day's effort for an honest day's pay." As Smith Barney said so well, "Make your money the old-fashioned way: earn it."

13. Co-workers who develop more than a work relationship tend to make the workplace fun. In a sense, because of the ties found there, persons begin to look forward to another day at the office, factory, foundry, plant or worksite.
    We should consider ourselves blessed by the rungs we have climbed on the economic ladder, especially given the advantages our foreparents didn't have. Work should tax us, but if we quit because of the pressure, we risk all that we have acquired.

14. The ability to talk and exchange ideas during lunch breaks will lessen the pressure of certain jobs. One good idea may be to try to find ways to compliment others on the job, in light of the fact that we all need a "lift."

15. One of the biggest problems in any work environment is the mixing of business with pleasure. In practical terms, this forbids dating fellow employees. Never allow your advancement to be interpreted as a reflection of dating the boss. Few such relationships last, and you will end up looking for employment rather than the boss or supervisor.

16. In a corporate setting, where there are opportunities for rising quickly, a woman particularly should not date her immediate supervisor as it will lead to rumors as to the "real" (with a wink) reasons for her success.

17. More and more, the issue of "sexual harassment" rears its head. One should be careful about what is said and suggested on the job. No matter the side one came down on during the Clarence Thomas-Anita Hill debate, the

allegations, nevertheless, will haunt both for the rest of their lives.

18. In the arena of the "politically correct," there is an entirely new lexicon of terms which seek not to offend any group, race, or gender. In many companies, employees are required to attend "sensitivity training" seminars so as to familiarize themselves with the new ways of addressing fellow "associates" in the workplace.

19. In lieu of raises, many companies are being bought by the employees, with the result being a greater stake in the direction the conglomerate takes. Along with "stock options" and more, one can really feel a place in the company to which he/she gives daily loyalty.

20. Not surprisingly, as with all of American society, the workplace has become increasingly more violent. Stress has taken its toll. Often, in the news, we hear of a disgruntled, former employee who returns to exact punishment on a hated supervisor. When guns enter the mix, innocent fellow employees may be victimized.

21. The NAFTA and GATT agreements will make it easier for large corporations to trade with others on the world stage. An accompanying downside, however, may be that "cheap labor" in other countries may make it more cost effective to produce overseas, the result being a wholesale loss of jobs here in America.

22. Somewhat related to the foregoing, the large influx of "illegal aliens" will mean the loss of jobs for native-born Americans, even as many realize that the newly-arrived will take on jobs that traditionally went to low-skilled blacks (hotel maids, waiters, etc.).

23. The health care reform movement of the mid 90s was a scare to many because it, no doubt, would have called for some type of "employer mandate," whereby the company owner would have had to pick up a major portion of the health insurance of all employees.

Clearly, the above represents but a "thumbnail sketch" of some of what one should know about the major trends and changes along the path to career advancement.

Let me add a few comments about what one should also read in order to remain current and on "the cutting edge." You need to know what those in the know plan to do, before it occurs, so that you are not left behind. Information is the key concept here.

Reading List
Forbes
Wall Street Journal
US News/World Report
Time
Fortune
Black Enterprise
Business Week
Newsweek

Contacts for Advancement

Conventions
Seminars
Classes for Training
Networking

What About Your Resume

   A. Above all, be honest about educational background / work history
   B. List major responsibilities in previous positions
   C. State capabilities in a concise fashion
   D. Be prepared with both personal and professional references
   E. Be forthright about previous employment (why no longer there)
   F. Have your resume done in a professional manner

Salary Questions

   A. Know what the market will bear
   B. Be forthright about what you expect

C. Ask for a raise when you deserve one
D. What you agree to you must abide by
E. Know the difference between it and "fringe benefits":
  - overtime pay?
  - vacation time/sick leave/paid or unpaid
  - medical/dental/pension plan of the company
  - life insurance
  - OSHA regulations
  - EEOC possibilities for redress of complaints
  - COLAs (cost of living adjustments)
  - job stability/seniority
  - profit-sharing

A career should differ from a job in that one has gone to college and/or graduate school for the former, while the latter expects one to merely complete a function. A career may not be exactly what one desires initially, but get all the knowledge you possibly can before moving on.

Just out of college, most people will move into a career because of recruitment from corporate representatives. This may or may not be the best move, as many will learn later. Eager persons in the career pool may find that the promise of a recruiter does not hold up in the glare of reality.

Also, one will have to be prepared for mobility if a career opens in the sector of an IBM, ARCO, Coca-Cola, AT&T, GE and more. To advance in such corporations, one must possess affability and be ready to make frequent moves, often to different sectors of America.

More than ever, we need, as African-Americans, more doctors, lawyers, dentists, specialists, teachers, counselors, entrepreneurs, real estate brokers, professors, computer technicians and other professionals. To get to these responsible positions, one must be prepared. When Blacks take on non-traditional roles in corporate America, Fortune 500 companies, it allows the nation to see what all persons, given a chance, are capable of.

THE MATTER OF MY MONEY

Perhaps the most important barometer of a Christian's witness to the Lordship of Jesus Christ can be viewed in the context of his/her position on money matters. Our financial resources and the disbursement of them indicates our true spiritual posture. In other words, the Bible tells of the bond between our treasure and the heart (Matthew 6:21).

As a Christian Single, you may feel as if how you spend, when you spend, where you spend, and on what you spend, fall within your personal discretion, since, after all, you have no mate to "answer to." Such reasoning is faulty, however, in light of how every believer is accountable, first, to God for the choices of life, including those having to do with money matters.

At its heart, then, this chapter will consider money as a spiritual matter, rather than a financial one.

What do you really treasure? What really has value in your life? What do you spend lavishly upon? These and other questions must be answered, with a practical consideration of the teachings from Scripture with reference to your money.

To be sure, there are mild objections to the idea of raising money. In the main, such objections would follow a certain pattern: Why is the use of my money anybody's business? Why do preachers always talk about money? Can't I just go to church once without being asked to give? Didn't Jesus say money is evil?

In the course of this chapter, we hope to confront these objections, with the hope of providing a clear analysis of the Master's teaching, whereby you may be able to determine what God seeks as He comments on your money. Money matters, and it matters to God!

In view of the brevity of time we have to live, along with the certainty of leaving behind so much at our departure in death, we would do well to reconsider our policy toward our possessions. (As a pastor, I have led many funeral processionals to the gravesite. Not once have I witnessed a "U-Haul" for the goods of the deceased among the many automobiles making their way there. Truly, "you can't take it with you!" Someone will have it all after you have gone.)

Are we stewards or owners? Can any item be spoken of as ours? Can we assert a total right to goods, products, commodities, things and more?

A wise person, grounded in godliness knows that, "<u>In the beginning God created the heavens and the earth</u>," so as to establish divine ownership. The Creator, from nothing, created everything. He is, therefore, absolute in His owning of all there is.

Moreover, such a person has a stubborn faith which issues forth in "<u>The earth is the Lord's, and all it contains, the world, and those who dwell in it</u>" (Psalm 24:1).

Therefore, <u>we must begin with the critical distinction of absolute ownership resident in the Creator</u>.

Several important propositions flow from such biblical dogmatism.

1. As Creator, Owner and Sustainer, God has absolute sovereignty.
2. Nowhere is there written or oral record of God's ownership ever being transferred. Man has no "deed of sale" whereby he/she can claim subsequent ownership.
3. Despite the unique position of man in relation to all other creation, man is not only himself a creature, but also a possession of the Creator. Consequently, whatever man has or is belongs to God!
4. At best, man is a "<u>steward</u>," or "one assigned to watch over the affairs of another for a pre-determined period,

phase or era, during which time he/she is accountable to the owner."

Please find Matthew 25:14-30; Luke 12:37-48.

5. Jesus Christ is our best example of a perfect steward in all areas of life; thus He provides a fitting model for our behavior.

Refer to Luke 2:49b. Here we find a perfect example of the Master's sense of mission from the Father, to whom He would be both faithful and accountable.

Every believer will, likewise, be called before the Lord to fittingly "give account" of how he/she has used the gifts of the Lord.

6. Since man's fall in the Garden, inasmuch as God's reign was not given full recognition, an inverse relationship holds sway, as "things" now have dominion over man, rather than the reverse.

A. R. Fagan, writing in What the Bible Says About Stewardship, is to be commended for such an arresting insight as the one cited above.

A. Louis Patterson, one of America's finest expository preachers, gives a related word, when he says, "God made us 'human beings,' rather than 'human havers,' or 'human getters'."

7. An excellent barometer for gauging a person's true heart concern was shared by Christ in an epoch statement: "For where your treasure is, there will your heart be also" (Matthew 6:21).

In the context, if you "check out" my checkbook, you have a window into who I really am. Am I Mr. Visa? Brother American Express? Ms. High Car Note? Sister Neiman Marcus? or someone else?

8. A good steward must reevaluate all relationships, primarily the one with God. Is He owner? If so, all things change!

9. Christian stewardship, especially in giving of material resources, must follow a definite commitment.

Please turn to 2 Corinthians 8:5. "But they first gave

themselves to the Lord and to us by the will of the Lord."
When a person makes the "Lordship of Christ" the cornerstone of his/her existence, the result is a yielded life, where all belongs to Him, including and especially that most important of all matters, his/her money!

10. Reflective of genuine commitment, Christians give to the object of their love, following the pattern of the Lord. Read John 3:16. What a gracious and generous God we serve!

One can give without loving but he/she cannot love without giving.

Lately, many have engaged in conflict over the necessity of paying the tithe (10% of one's income) as a New Testament Christian.

It is argued, by the non-tither, that tithing was definitely an Old Testament concept, governed by the <u>Law</u>, completely without relevance to those who have accepted Christ by <u>Grace</u>. The contrast yet reigns.

Moreover, the non-tithers hold that the Christian should not be under an obligation to give a specified amount: His "freedom" in Christ, they point out, should govern the level of giving.

We must examine these positions in light of Scripture, because we may have a further complement to tithing, instead of a competing philosophy.

I wholeheartedly believe that we may find more places of understanding among tithers and Grace-Givers than we had previously thought.

11. <u>Why I believe in and practice tithing</u>.

    A. Jesus Christ endorsed tithing as normative giving for a believer.
       Read Matthew 23:23; Luke 14:42
       While endorsing the tithe, Christ calls upon His followers to also include weighty matters such as "justice and mercy and faithfulness."

    B. The Scriptures validate tithing for God's people.
       Read Genesis 14:20; Genesis 28:22; Leviticus 27:30;

Numbers 18:26

C. The Old Testament is just as relevant and authoritative for us today as it was "way back when."
Read Malachi 3:8-12.
Someone with wisdom has said, "The Old Testament is the New Testament concealed, while the New Testament is the Old Testament revealed."

D. God has provided for all my needs, as He promised. The blessings from God have been in many areas, far beyond financial reciprocity. Yet, I challenge anyone to give as the Master teaches in His Word. I know you will benefit in unimaginable ways!

12. <u>Words in favor of tithing</u>.
    A. Tithing is a tenth of one's income, financial increase by any means.
    B. Tithing is a debt, owed to God; it is not an offering.
    C. Tithing should be paid on time, each Sunday ("first day of the week").
    D. Nothing less than the tithe will satisfy the requirement.
    E. The tithe should be brought to the church ("storehouse").
    F. Tithing should take precedence over any other debts, bills.
    G. The non-tither has a curse upon him/her, for "robbery."

13. <u>Tithing is an excellent "starting point", but should be exceeded by a happy Christian</u>.
    "Grace" giving should be a means of exceeding the Law. If the Law says, "<u>You must pay 10% of income</u>," then Grace says, "<u>You may set the limit</u>."
    Tell me, friend, which category do you fit in?

14. God has an immutable law in the arena of giving: <u>sowing</u> and <u>reaping</u>.
    Read 2 Corinthians 9:6. Apply it to your life.

15. A willingness of heart, shown by a hilarious, cheerful, giddy spirit should characterize the Christian's attitude toward giving.

Read 2 Corinthians 9:7. Apply it to your daily living.

When one gives God's way, His promise involves enough to meet all needs and even an abundance.

Read 2 Corinthians 9:8-12. Apply this passage and believe the promise.

16. The ultimate goal in giving should always be the glory of God.

Read 2 Corinthians 9:13-15. Apply this text in all of life.

Finally, accept the advice of Dr. E.V. Hill, pastor and preacher of national stature, who holds that the pattern of stewardship should involve a tripartite division: "<u>Give some; Share some; and Save some</u>."

At the same time, we need to give some direction to those who genuinely yearn to grow in their giving to the Lord, through His church, evangelistic ministries, and various kingdom enterprises.

For such persons, the best advice may relate to how one gets out of debt, how one breaks the stranglehold of credit cards and consumerism.

First, one needs to sit down and think long and hard about the matter of money. The United States government has operated with a high debt for many years. The mid 90s have brought the Republicans to the fore in both houses of the United States Congress. One of their key programmatic thrusts is the "balanced budget" amendment. Simply stated, the government should only spend as much as it takes in from taxes. If the federal lawmakers have the good sense to call a halt to runaway spending, surely those who have the Spirit of God as their Leader should do likewise.

Second, as a practical matter, one may need to total up all the consumer debt, from all sources, in order to get an accurate sense of how much debt one owes. It may be astounding! It may run into the thousands. Remember, the major credit providers really never want you out of debt.

That's why so many get "pre-approved" cards, which only require a signature to acquire. As long as you pay that monthly $25 or $50, such credit guarantors will be satisfied. The result of such a payment plan is that you never get around to paying off the bill in full ("financial freedom").

Of course, the purchase of a home, or an automobile will fall outside the normal rules about heavy debt. But, many financial advisors/planners would even give helpful suggestions about the purchase of those.

One of the best Christian writers on the subject of biblical stewardship/debt counseling/financial planning is Larry Burkett. He has several fine books on various topics related to your money. I recommend that you acquire the books which fit your area of interest.

Third, the best way to get out of debt is to adopt a systematic plan to pay one credit card off, in entirety, and then begin working on another. What you save in interest will be in the thousands. Just as it took time to make the debt, it will take time to retire it. But, if you use a proven plan, the results will come.

Also, it will help to begin to paraphrase the old American Express tag line: "leave home without it." In other words, intentionally leave your credit cards at home, so as to prevent "impulse buying." Too many people spend without thinking of the long-term repercussions.

Fourth, one should develop a personal budget. It may seem daunting, or something that only economics majors could do, but the truth is that anybody who knows simple addition and subtraction can do it. There ought be two items: Income and Expenditures. Think of all the sources of income for a given month. Total them up. Multiply by the 12 months. This is your Annual Income. The other portion should total all expenditures for the month. Multiply by the 12 months. These are your Annual Expenditures.

The budget comes into focus, however, when you look at the list of expenditures, since most people cannot exert as much influence over their income (usually derived from weekly, bi-monthly, monthly compensation on the job). Everyone will need housing, transportation, food, insurance, clothing, personal items, and more to live each month. When preparing a budget, there are "fixed" costs (Mortgage, rent, utilities, car note, insurance, food, etc.) and then "discretionary" costs. You must look at what you spend on, and then decide what is essential and what is frivolous.

A budget is a practical way to gain a sense of direction, to develop spiritual discipline, master one's money, and to save for the future. Without a budget, one will be forever caught in a cycle of spending. Over and again, one will be frustrated and disillusioned by what seems a mountain of bills.

Finally, there are many who can help you clear up discrepancies on a credit report. There are three databases for reporting your credit history: TRW; Equifax; and Trans Union. You have the right to know what each agency has on file as to your history. This is what banks, credit companies, employers, and others see when they call up your social security number. You should obtain a copy of the report. If there are errors, you may be able to erase damaging data. Find out all you can about this area of your finances and act in the way that will assure you opportunities for financial flexibility.

Of course, these words are simply meant to stimulate your thinking in the arena of your personal finances. Since money is not really about the dollar, but about discipleship, you should definitely make these money matters an issue for prayer.

I can be dogmatic and direct about one item: when you are weighed down by financial concerns, it can lead to depression, frustration and agony. You may seek to be liberal in sharing, but when you're broke, it puts a drain on your spirit. The devil is the thief who desires to rob you of the joy of giving to further the causes of the Lord. Thus, you may need to be delivered in your personal finances, in the same way others may need it for a habit or an addiction.

HAGAR:
PORTRAIT OF A SINGLE MOTHER

The statistics are sobering for the number of one-parent families in America, and especially is the picture bleak among African-Americans, where a "matriarchal system" characterizes the majority of family units.

In other words, due to male abandonment of parental responsibility, divorces where children remain with their mothers, children borne out of wedlock who remain with their mothers, fathers who are imprisoned, and various reasons, black families, particularly, have females as heads of households.

We can see this trend in many ways, chiefly in the cycle of poverty as welfare rolls have a disproportionate number of single-parent families, largely of the African-American variety.

How do we as a church minister to these women, these families?

What are the concerns of these Single Adults, who happen to have one, two, three or more children to care for without male assistance?

Are there biblical models for coping with the pressures and problems of Single Parents?

What emotional, psychological and spiritual effects will ensue from being reared in a home headed by a Single Adult?

These and other questions must be faced, if there is to be healing and wholeness in the Body of Christ, to say nothing of an outreach to the unsaved mothers who have bitterness, anger and resentment toward the circumstances which have brought about their present plight.

Genesis 16 furnishes a story full of pathos as a family

seeks to put into perspective a wonderful promise from God, one which produces joy in its pronouncement and incredulity in its fulfillment.

That God would bless the nation from the seed of Abram (Abraham) brings great joy, but that Sarai (Sarah), who like her husband Abram is past the child-bearing years, will be the mother who brings a measure of incredulity.

Sarah "laughs" at such an astounding promise from glory; yet, our God is abundantly able to perform and thus validate what He declares!

How will God do it?

1. Before Jehovah has an opportunity to stretch the faith of this couple, like most of us do today, they figure out a means by which they may "help" the Lord.
2. According to the customs of that day, a slave could join with her master, and with the full knowledge of the mistress (Sarah, here), become the "surrogate" mother of a child formed from such a relationship.
3. The marital relationship originally designed by God to include two persons now entails three: Abram, Sarai and Hagar.
4. Up until the time of conception, there seems to be harmony and gaiety; only to be interrupted by the near impossibility of "two queens on the same throne."

These introductory comments open the way for a fuller discussion of the topic of the single-parent lifestyle. May we learn from the story found in Genesis 16 and Genesis 21.

At several points one will find an Abram (Abraham) who comes off as less than the shining biblical patriarch; also Sarai (Sarah) will be shown as one more in touch with her femininity than her beliefs in Yahweh; and Hagar will be seen as both victim and victimizer.

(That God used all of these persons in His plan for the redemption of humanity must stand as a given. That Abraham

was a man of faith, though he experienced doubt and frustration like us all, must be kept in mind. That the ugly incidents from the Middle East, to this very moment, stem from this arrangement should guide our thinking and make us all the more careful in our dealings because a "moment of pleasure can mean a lifetime of pain.")

5. Abram allowed himself the pleasures of this arrangement without a sense of responsibility for the slave Hagar as a person. - Verse 6

6. An implicit order to leave the family dwelling comes from Sarai to the pregnant slave girl. This quick arrangement has blown up in the faces of all involved.
   - God delivers on His promises in His own way!
   - The "biological clock" is in the Master's hand.
   - Love triangles never work! Somebody flunks geometry!

7. An unwise decision leads to deception as Hagar must now make it as best as she can. What should have been a joint matter is now her's exclusively: (the child and his rearing).
   - "Welfare" cuts may mean "do-your-share"
   - In most cases, the mother is left with the children
   - The mid 90s Republican takeover may mean the end of welfare "as we know it."
   - The general programs, Head Start, AFDC, meals for children, and more are threatened by budget cuts.

8. God loves, and thus never leaves, His own, as He comes in the form of an inquiring angel. - Verses 7-8
   - The need to analyze soberly one's predicament - 2 questions
   - 1 million teens become pregnant in America each year.
   - The largest percentage of all births to African American mothers occurs among those who are unmarried.
   - Because of God's concern, the church must be concerned by establishing a ministry of outreach and affirmation.

9. Appalling, indeed, must have been the angel's words to Hagar as he advises her to return to Abram and Sarai's home for the birth of the baby. This, however, fits into the divine plan for her life.

10. The decision and the deception now provoke a dilemma as she makes the trek back to the place of humiliation.
    • "How can I make the best of a bad situation?"
    • "Can I look forward to a husband and father to my children?"
    • "What will life hold for me?"

11. After some time, the child is born, and grows to become a problem for all concerned, since, by this time, God has fulfilled His promise by bringing forth Isaac (Genesis 21).

12. Not surprisingly, Abraham (though with God's directive) again puts Hagar out of the family dwelling place.

13. Hagar and the boy are in a desert, both literally and figuratively.
    • They wander aimlessly, as the water and food are gone.
    • The ostracism of a single woman and a fatherless boy.
    • School friends can be cruel when Ishmael has no one to bring to "Father-Son" games.
    • Water (money) runs out often when one has to be the bread-winner for the whole family.

14. Since the decision has lead to the deception, which brought about the dilemma, we now see her desperation.

15. Out of the midst of her troubles, God speaks words of comfort, hope and love.
    • No one gets outside the knowledge of a loving Father.
    • Since Hagar and Ishmael have no provider, they get a Greater One.
    • Don't allow financial need to cause a loss in morality.
    • Spiritual integrity means waiting for God!

16. While still in the desert, God reveals a bit of an answer.
    - verse 19
    • There will be water for your thirst.

- Big Brothers come to the aid of fatherless boys.
- The Boy Scouts, Cub Scouts and YMCA teach values for living.
- A strong Children's Ministry strengthens the family.

As an illustration, God is "Jehovah Jireh," or our providential provider, in that He gives favor before those who can help us. In such case, it may the loan officer who initially turns one down for a home loan. As a single mother you then go to your cramped apartment, and take time out to pray. When God speaks, He moves the loan officer to reconsider. Against his better judgment, he calls you back. The house is yours! God moves in mysterious ways!

Conclusion

The Reverend Jesse Jackson tells the story from his own life of being the product of a single-parent home. He faced the jeering of his peers because there were ugly rumors as to who his father was. Shame came to him through no fault of his own. Society branded him a "loser."

Yet, like Ishmael, one can never give up! God ultimately has the last word, as evidenced by Jackson's spectacular run for the presidency of the United States:

Don't give up on Ishmael! He will be a college president!

Don't give up on Ishmael! He will write books and lead people!

Don't give up on Ishmael! He will preach the gospel of Christ!

Don't give up on Ishmael! He will serve this present age!

Don't give up on Ishmael! He will use all the talents given by God!

Words of Challenge

As a Single Parent, may I leave you with a few words to help you meet the challenge of your life, in a practical way.

    A. If juveniles are to be taught, you will do the teaching or else they will fall prey to gangs, drugs, etc.

B. Try to teach values and principles (honesty, reaping and sowing) that will remain long after your words have been forgotten.

C. Take courage in three single parents made so because of the killings of the civil rights struggle in America during the 1960s:
   - Myrlie Evers, (widow of Medgar — several children), went on to chair the NAACP.
   - Betty Shabazz (widow of Malcolm X — many children) earned a doctorate degree.
   - Coretta King, (widow of Martin — four children), led a humanitarian foundation.

D. If you desire it, you have a biblical right to remarry or to find a Christian mate and step-father for your child(ren).
   I submit several biblical references to undergird my point: Titus 2:4-5; 2 Timothy 5:14; 1 Corinthians 7:39-40.

E. As you know already, to be a single parent means a duality of responsibility, as you must be mother (nurture and support) and father (discipline and direction).

F. Share your perspective with other women and men who must face life as single parents, in the context of spiritual maturity, taking the Bible and good Christian books as your guide.

G. Develop a "support group" within your church fellowship by asking the pastor of your church for the chance to join together for prayer, Bible study, sharing of needs and more on a weekly basis or bi-monthly basis.

H. Pray for the ability to be a good parent! God will make it happen!

DRUG ABUSE

An ominous crisis has engulfed the land, with a pervasive threat to our very existence as a people. This crisis has no historical equivalent. This crisis ruins families, decimates communities, annihilates churches, and wreaks havoc by the thousands.

The crisis to which I refer is DRUG ABUSE.

It is the scourge of a generation, yet reeling from the permissiveness of earlier times. It portends the loss of the young and able-bodied. It is the greatest threat since widespread disease, plague and all other forms of mass death.

That drug abuse kills so many African-Americans makes it tempting to ask whether this is part of a plan for genocide for the race; yet, the equally disturbing fact that African-Americans are providing drugs to their brothers and sisters lets us know that there is no master plan for the extinction of the race.

Pick up any newspaper, turn on any radio and one discovers the extent of the problem of drug abuse: professional ballplayers, actors, doctors, politicians, singers, the rich, the famous, the poor, the white, and all others.

Anybody and everybody has fallen within the last few years!

Single Adults, perhaps caught in a spiral of loneliness and despair, are particularly susceptible to the allurement of drugs, because they seem to offer an escape from the hurt and frustration.

Add to this the way in which popular culture shows neon signs all tied to the boost given by various narcotics. Is it any wonder that so many have fallen by the "wayside"?

Drugs come in many varieties, yet I want to concentrate on a few of the most popular in the contemporary setting: Marijuana; Amphetamines; Barbiturates; PCP; Heroin; Cocaine; Crack; Freebase; Valium; and a host of others, including Alcoholic Beverages.

According to Dr. Ronald Siegel, author of "Intoxication - Life in Pursuit of Artificial Paradise," the "motivation to achieve an altered state of mood or consciousness is a 'fourth drive,' as much a part of the human condition as sex, thirst and hunger."

If he is right, then, we will have to tell the drug addict about One who not only speaks against the act, but who also can change the nature!

Since a drug abuser is given over to external stimuli, he/she must hear the clarion words from on high, "Therefore if any man/woman is in Christ, he/she is a new creature; the old things are passed away; behold, new things have come." (2 Corinthians 5:17).

This "new creature" has a new life. The old way of addiction is gone. With the aid of the Holy Spirit, such a person can begin to walk in new life, this time with a heavenly partner.

Thus, at the outset, I must assert that the hope is a new life in Christ!

Yet, we are still haunted by a nemesis so virulent and acute until the United States has established the White House Office of Drug Control Policy, headed by an African American, Lee Brown. As "Drug Czar" we have an overall coordinator for the declared "war on drugs."

In a recent poll, conducted by the Gallup organization, 27% of Americans view drugs as a major problem and 62% express a willingness to pay additional taxes to combat them.

Furthermore, one must consider the relation of drugs and money. The situation is such that ships and planes carry the cocaine into America, while billions flow from this country. Several countries in South America, such as Columbia and Bolivia, export their deadly crop to America.

From "Miami Vice" fiction to Los Angeles fact, we know intuitively of the high profits to be derived from drugs such as cocaine. The newscasts repeatedly describe million dollar seizures of drugs. As the police confiscate tons of illegal narcotics, it seems as if untold tons make their way to thousands of nostrils and veins.

1. <u>Why do people abuse drugs?</u>
   A. The pleasure of the "high" - temporary euphoria
   B. A part of the "cool," "down," "hip," "jet-set" lifestyle
   C. The need to cope with life's frustrations - "make it over"
   D. The pull of peers - "You should try this, man."
   E. "I can handle a bit of this" syndrome - myth of moderation
   F. A foolish fascination - "I'll try anything once."
   G. The lack of moral absolutes - "Who and what says its wrong?"
   H. You name it!

2. <u>The nature of drug addiction</u>
   A. Increased Dosage over time to maintain "high"
   B. Insulation from Family, Friends
   C. The Loss of Weight
   D. Noticeable Forgetfulness, Lack of Coordination
   E. Willingness to spend all for drug of choice - stealing if needed
   F. Drastic change in Moods, Behavior
3. <u>"Costs" of drug addiction</u>
   A. Family Breakdown - wives/husbands, children are big losers
   B. Extended Family Embarrassment - grandparents, cousins, others
   C. Loss of Productivity - lateness for work; can't concentrate
   D. Decay of Society - "pillars have fallen" - Psalm 11
   E. Control of the Mind - the real battle is fought there!

F. Respect for God - an addict has no thoughts of Him
G. The Deterioration of Life - everything goes out the
    window

In light of the above, many will throw their hands up in anguish, as if to say, "With such daunting depths of a situation, what can we really do to make a difference."

Before I make some suggestions for the amelioration of this deadly scenario of chemical dependency, allow me to paint the picture a bit bleaker, with the hope that when the light comes it will shine brighter!

A conservative estimate has approximately $100 billion per year now spent on cocaine. This figure represents what is spent on the purchase of the drug. This takes in all the small drug transactions on the street corner, on the school campus, down the block, and everywhere. The toll we yet seek to tally has to do with broken lives, buried dreams, snuffed-out potential, and the wholesale waste in the culture. The number of abusers grows every year. Several million have already experimented with many dangerous forms of drugs. It is the shame of the day.

The war on drugs must be fought at both the level of <u>drug availability</u> (Minorities who use have no planes or boats to bring it in) and chemical desire (get at the attraction of the "high"). The former must be addressed by the government, while the latter is an issue for the individual and the moral institutions, such as the Church. We in the Body of Christ should be prepared with a word of hope and redemption.

Drug abuse must not be allowed to have the final say in the direction of our families, homes and communities. What the federal, state, and local governments cannot do, we in the family of God must come forth with the wherewithal to stem this scourge.

I know that even as many programs, 12-step ones, such as Nacre-anon and Free-N-One are up and running in many ministry-minded church fellowships, the need is still yet great. We need more churches who will be willing to engage in a break from the traditional, to meet the growing necessity of providing for the hurting, the sick, the troubled, and those groping for hope. When they turn to drugs, it is the cry of despair.

The redemptive church will not be deaf to such cries!

A word to the drug abuser, the chemically-addicted: You must reach out for help. There is a lifeline back. God cares about you, even if you assume that others don't care. You only need to "get up" and seek out places of help and hope. There are excellent resources near you, in any area of the country.

The way back is long and hard. You will fall in your comeback. You may relapse. You may go back to old habits. But, always note that God is waiting and willing to walk that long road with you. If you need to find a program, or a recovering addict, look for that assistance in the local church family.

The Church is not a perfect place, but it is a family of persons who share a common reality: all are deeply concerned about the hurting, as all in the church have a "sin" problem, one which we have taken to one above us, known as Jesus Christ. He died for your sin, your drug problem, your lack of discipline, whatever, and He will be the "lifeline" back to the Father.

Whatever you do, please don't give up hope!

Moreover, hear the voice of a distinguished sociologist, Jerome Skolnick, professor at UC Berkeley Law School: "But jobless youth...are not rational cost-benefit calculators, partly because the threat is not entirely credible, but mostly because they have few alternatives. The threat of imprisonment can be assimilated by even a rational risk aggressor who has little to lose and much to gain by a life of crime, especially the entrepreneurial activity of drug marketing."

There we have the words of a "secular" authority who agrees that even putting all the drug addicts in jail will not solve the problem.

4. <u>What are some possible solutions?</u>
   A. Family Response - love and affirm the "sick" person;
   B. Church Challenge - ministry of outreach;
   C. Societal Concern - not to condemn, nor to condone, but to confront;
   D. Re-establish the moral wrong of drugs - the Bible says so!;
   E. Work Against the Demand - find out the whys of desire for drugs;
   F. Work Against the Supply - too much comes across the borders of USA;
   G. Counseling, Treatment Centers - there are hospitals everywhere;

The drug scourge will not be dealt with until we muster up the resolve, to take personal responsibility for those in our families who need our help, in order to lead productive, healthy lives. It is a challenge we have been slow to take up, but the "human casualties" make this a war we must fight!

In our families, we must reach out to those who are addicted and let them know that there is hope. In Christ, there is abundant hope.

<u>Drugs may be an opportunity for the church of Jesus Christ to show that He can make a radical difference in human endeavors.</u>

WHERE CHRISTIAN SINGLE ADULTS GATHER

Single Adults are characterized by <u>motivation</u> and <u>mobility</u>. If they have a good reason, they will go certain places. Though parents and friends may desire otherwise, the reality teaches us that Single Adults don't sit for very long. Perhaps many would make less disastrous choices if they did slow down, yet conventional wisdom says that, in light of the decisions with which they are faced, it does not seem as if they will overnight become sedentary.

Having said that, where can we find Single Adults for friendship, companionship, courtship and relationship?

A. In morning worship - with a pretty dress/conservative suit on;

B. At a Church Convention, Seminar, Revival - spiritual values;

C. Visit Another Congregation - tell the Usher where to seat you;

D. Evening Classes at Local College/University - learn as you yearn;

E. Sporting Events - get season seats;

F. Restaurants - get a big table and look like you want company;

G. Health/Fitness Clubs - be healthy and happy;

H. Weddings - festive occasions bring out the best in people;

I. Political Rallies/Campaigns - "let's stuff these envelopes;

J. Flights/Tour Groups - ask the boarding agent to put you next to him/her;

K. Carwash - you have a captive friend;

L. Movies/Plays/Readings - a display of pop culture;

M. Museums/Exhibits - "what do you see in that painting?";

N. Singles Ministry Meeting - shared values;

O. Supermarket - "I just hate to freeze all this extra food";

P. Cleaners/Laundry - comment on their clothes;

Q. Christian Socials - invite 10 Single Adults;

R. Birthday Dinner - food and friendship;

DEVELOPING A CHRISTIAN SINGLES MINISTRY

Any Church which seriously seeks to reach the most creative, most talented, most available group in society should attempt to organize a Christian Singles Ministry.

The size and structure of the ministry are not as critical as having one which seeks to take in the multi-faceted interests of the group. A practical note: stress spiritual, start small, and stay simple. If you follow these general rules, you will gain new converts and produce a healthy example of discipleship.

Key Concepts:

1. The ministry should always be Christ-centered. He is the focus around which all things revolve;
2. The ministry should be comprehensive to be effective. Allow the Singles to bring their concerns, rather than dictating to them what the concerns are (paternalism);
3. The ministry should be person-centered. Let it be known that individuals are critical to the operation;
4. The ministry should lead those involved to meet others' needs through Christian service;
5. The ministry should be needs-oriented. Find a need and fill it. People tend to gather where their needs are being met;
6. The ministry should be holistic in nature, centering on the development of disciples;
7. The ministry should embrace spiritual, intellectual, physical and social aspects;
8. The ministry should be an integral part of the life of the church and its total ministry;
9. The ministry should be "with" and not "to" Singles. Who "owns" the ministry is vital;

The best beginning is to call together the available

singles in the church. In a relaxed time, ask about their interest in an on-going Singles Ministry. Seek out a leader, pray for guidance from the Lord. Set out some of the concerns (perhaps some of the chapters of this booklet), plan an event which will be exciting and enjoyable. Invite other Singles Ministry groups from other churches in the area, interface with such groups, and carry forth the work.

Clearly, the early steps are critical. But I caution all to allow the mistakes to occur, so long as you learn not to repeat the more deadly ones. There are very few perfect ministries, so you can be creative, innovative and unusual.

Most important is that your ministry be one where biblical discipleship, stressing the daily Lordship of Jesus Christ in the lives of all Christian singles is cultivated and maintained by all participants.

Keep the ministry vibrant by focusing on the positive, which is possible by adopting the Word of God as the guide. With support from books, tapes, lectures, conferences, gatherings, and times of loving support.

For any church, the Singles Ministry can provide a much-needed impetus for all other ministries, as it is peopled by committed, caring, adventuresome, upwardly-mobile, go-getters, who, by and large, want their lives to mean something. Therefore, any Single's ministry which is dull, lifeless, irrelevant, boring or traditional is bound to fail.

The tools for building a strong ministry are available to you. Each person can make the Ministry soar to heights unimaginable. I trust that this material will assist in that regard. (The bibliography will give further resources.)

THE FUTURE

???

The facts have been given to you, Christian Single Adult.

Now, some hard choices are before you. You, and only you, will be called upon to develop your life with God.

I can only say to you that the challenges will grow each day. These pages do not cover options, but obligations which you must face today and in the future.

<u>The basis for your decision-making should be the authoritative Word of the Lord, who speaks words of assurance and teaches the truth which will set us free from the shackles of ignorance.</u>

In the days ahead, as you move towards greater responsibilities, you will need some familiarity with the topics and concerns of Single Adults both in the church and those outside.

<u>Whatever the future holds, make sure that your anchor is Christ</u>! Jesus Christ is the only answer!

Learn from life and love life because there is so much to gain by being a keen observer of all that God does in the last few years of the 20th Century, as we stand on the threshold of the 21st. This is a great time to be alive. God is at work in the world in a marvelous manner. Grab hold of life and enjoy it to the fullest. Don't let any "joy-stealer" take what God has for you. (Your future is so bright, you need shades to handle it!)

Whatever you do, Christian Single Adult, know that God's calling is one of "faithfulness" in the state you are (Philippians 4), because you, like Paul and all believers: "You can do all things through Christ who strengthens you" (Philippians 4:13).

May the love of Christ be with you always.

BIBLIOGRAPHY

Barna, George. *The Frog in the Kettle*. Ventura, CA: Regal Books, 1990.

_____. *User Friendly Churches*. Ventura, CA: Regal Books, 1991.

_____. *The Power of Vision*. Ventura, CA: Regal Books, 1992.

Cornwall, Judson. *Leaders Eat What You Serve*. Shippensburg, PA: Destiny Image Publishers, 1988.

Cotham, Perry C., editor. *Christian Social Ethics*. Grand Rapids, MI: Baker Book House, 1979.

Crawford, Dan R., compiler, *Single Adults-Resource and Recipients for Revival*. Nashville, TN: Broadman Press, 1985.

Fagan, A. R. *What the Bible Says About Stewardship*. Nashville, TN: Convention Press, 1976.

Fleming, Jean. *Between Walden and the Whirlwind*. Colorado Springs, CO: NAVPRESS, 1985.

Getz, Gene A. *The Measure of a Woman*. Ventura, CA: Regal Books, 1977.

Gray, John. *Men are from Mars, Women are from Venus*. New York, NY: HarperCollins, 1992.

Guernsey, Dennis B. *A New Design for Family Ministry*. Elgin, IL: David C. Cook Publishing, 1982.

Hershey, Terry. *Young Adult Ministry*. Loveland, CO: Group Books, 1986.

_____. *Go Away, Come Closer*. Dallas, TX: Word Publishing, 1990.

Hocking, David and Carole. *Good Marriages Take Time*. Eugene, OR: Harvest House Publishers, 1984.

_____. *Marrying Again.* Eugene, OR Harvard House Publishers.

Hopson, Derek S. and Darlene Powell. *Friends, Lovers and Soulmates: A Guide to Better Relationships Among Black Men and Women*. New York: Simon & Schuster, 1993.

Koons, Carolyn A. and Michael J. Anthony. *Single Adult*

Passages. Grand Rapids,MI: Baker Book House, 1991.

LaHaye, Tim and Beverly. _The Act of Marriage_. Grand Rapids, MI: Zondervan, 1976.

MacDonald, Gordon. _Magnificent Marriage_. Wheaton, IL: Tyndale, 1976.

_____. _Ordering Your Private World_. Nashville, TN: Thomas Nelson, 1984.

_____. _Restoring Your Spiritual Passion_. Nashville, TN: Thomas Nelson, 1986.

_____. _Rebuilding Your Broken World_. Nashville, TN: Thomas Nelson, 1988.

_____. _Forging A Real World Faith_. Nashville, TN: Thomas Nelson, 1989.

Mace, David and Vera. _What's Happening to Clergy Marriages_. Nashville, TN: Abingdon Press, 1980.

Matson, T. B. with William M. Tillman, Jr. _The Bible and Family Relations_. Nashville, TN: Broadman Press, 1983.

National Single Adult Ministries Resource Directory 1991/92.

Pearson, Bud and Kathy. _Single Again: Remarrying for the Right Reasons_. Ventura, CA: Regal Books, 1985.

Schaller, Lyle E. _It's A Different World!_ Nashville, TN: Abingdon, 1987.

Vaughan, Diane. _Uncoupling: Turning Points in Intimate Relationships_. New York, NY: Oxford University Press, 1986.

Williams, Don. _The Bond That Breaks: Will Homosexuality Split the Church?_ Los Angeles, CA: BIM, 1978.

Wright, H. Norman. _So You're Getting Married_. Ventura, CA: Regal Books, 1985.

_____. _Before You Say I Do_. Eugene, OR: Harvest House Publishers.

AUTHOR'S PROFILE

THE REV. JARVIS L. COLLIER

This native of Los Angeles, California, youngest of a family of four, comes forth with a gift for communicating the truth of the Word, in power, for the edification of the Church of the Lord Jesus Christ.

At present, God has chosen to utilize the dynamic voice of this man of God in several capacities: Pastor of the Fellowship Baptist Church, Los Angeles, California; Evangelist for several Revivals across America; Singles Conference Leader; Writer, The Informer, National Baptist Convention Board of Christian Education; Board Member, "One Church, One Child" (Black Adoptions) and more.

Pastor Collier is a graduate of the University of California, Los Angeles (UCLA), and the Fuller Theological Seminary, along with having done graduate study at Southwestern Baptist Theological Seminary. He has a sharp mind and a dedicated heart for the theological and practical dimensions of ministry.

This "Renaissance Man" is well-traveled, an avid reader, a prolific writer, and a tireless champion for the extension of the kingdom of God, in the hearts of humanity.